Stratification and Soci...
Studies in British Society

Stratification and Social Inequality;
Studies in British Society

Edited
by
Alan Warde and Nicholas Abercrombie

Framework Press Educational Publishers Ltd.
Parkfield
Greaves Road
LANCASTER
LA1 4TZ

First published 1994

ISBN 1 85008 069 0

**Stratification and Social Inequality;
Studies in British Society**

A catalogue record for the pack is available from the
British Library

Typeset by Blackpool Typesetting Services Ltd., Blackpool

Printed at Alden Press Limited,
Oxford and Northampton, Great Britain

Cover Design by John Angus

Table of Contents

Notes on Contributors

Nicholas Abercrombie – Professor of Sociology, University of Lancaster

Lisa Adkins – Lecturer in Sociology, University of the West of England

Paul Bagguley – Lecturer in Sociology, University of Leeds

Dawn Burton – Director of Postgraduate Training Course in Social Sciences, University of Sheffield

Mariam Fraser – Postgraduate Research Student, Sociology Department, University of Lancaster

Ken Hahlo – Senior Lecturer in Sociology, Bolton Institute of Higher Education

John Hartley – Postgraduate Research Student, Sociology Department, University of Lancaster

Colin Hay – Research Officer, Sociology Department, University of Lancaster

Celia Lury – Lecturer in Sociology, University of Lancaster

Michael Savage – Senior Lecturer in Sociology, University of Keele

Roger Walters – Teaching Fellow, Sociology Department, University of Lancaster

Alan Warde – Reader in Sociology, University of Lancaster

Anne Witz – Lecturer in Social Policy, University of Birmingham

Introduction

The principal aim of this book is to describe some important recent empirical, sociological studies of social inequality in Britain. Each chapter is written to a rough formula, placing an empirical study in its intellectual and historical context, describing the methods used in the investigation, summarising key findings, and giving a brief résumé of critical evaluations of the work. Each provides valuable information about sociological methods and the most recent research findings on key themes in the sociology of stratification in Britain.

Readers might use the chapters to discover what is in a particular recent study; to obtain an overview of recent empirical research in the general area of the sociology of stratification; to consider a series of examples of the way that evidence is linked to social scientific conclusions; and to evaluate different methods of data collection and analysis.

Each chapter has three objectives:

1. to introduce new empirical material on important topics not yet available in popular textbooks;
2. to reproduce materials – tables, verbatim passages from interviews, etc., appearing in the chapters and their appendices – which will help the reader appreciate the character of the evidence used to support the book's conclusions;
3. to give as an impartial an evaluation as possible of the studies under review. Our authors have consulted the full range of published reflection on the books discussed, often using book reviews in the major sociological journals. In cases where there has been little published commentary, usually where the studies are very recent, authors offer their own critical judgments. However, throughout, the aim has been to offer a 'plain' account, trying to avoid prejudging for the reader the strengths and the limitations of each study.

The reason for pursuing this third objective is that we hope the book will be used by students as a device for learning and practising the exercise of critical judgment about sociological research. Consequently, each chapter stands alone and there has been no attempt

1

to construct an integrated account of the social processes examined. We anticipate that chapters will be read separately and not necessarily in the order printed. This is a resource book rather than a textbook. Nevertheless, taken together, two important, integrating themes, one substantive, the other methodological, can be traced through the chapters.

First, much insight can be gained into the current state of social inequality in Britain, a topic of immense personal and public concern. The concept of stratification conveys a notion of the hierarchical ranking of social groups. Its sociological study refers to more than simply social difference. Rather it implies the identification of inequalities – of material resources, of prestige and of institutional power – that may be considered in some ways unjust, illegitimate and avoidable. In other words, inequalities, as opposed to differences, are potentially matters generating structured social conflict that, in certain circumstances, may entail political intervention for its elimination or management.

A principal theme of the analysis of stratification in Britain has been the role of social class. Once widely accepted as the principal dimension of inequality and the prime cause of political alignments, class came to be considered by many in the 1980s as having a much diminished importance in the understanding of structured inequality. Some sociologists have vigorously contested this conclusion, arguing that class differences remain primary. Other scholars have identified alternative sources of systematic social division. Most of these have concentrated on gender and ethnicity as the key dimensions. But also under consideration have been some new divisions, for instance around consumption, and the persistence or revival of some older sources of division, like religious affiliation (as in Northern Ireland, for example). Other sociologists have merely discerned greater and greater fragmentation within the UK population, such that major lines of division, and patterns of inequality, have dissolved as collective social struggles have given way to personal competition and private projects.

The evidence of the studies examined here offers examples of all these approaches and arguments. The conclusions one might draw are that class remains a very important division in Britain, since class position continues to affect social and political behaviour and the distribution of material resources between generations. However, other divisions also run very deep. For example, differences in social experiences and resources between men and women are shown to be fundamental and to derive from various sources. Men co-operate to exclude women from privileged positions within organizations. Labour market segmentation, effectively the reservation of certain, better paid, jobs for men, persists. The continued attribution of domestic and child-rearing responsibilities to women further restricts their access to careers and positions of power and influence. There is thus a case for maintaining that the pattern of gender inequality can be described in terms of a system of patriarchy – domination of women by men – that constitutes a social division deeper and more pervasive than that arising from class location.

To complicate matters, these dimensions of inequality co-exist, inter-penetrate and contaminate each other. Thus, for example, there are differences among women, between those belonging to different ethnic groups, age groups and social classes. The same holds for classes and ethnic groups which are internally differentiated. Experiences of such categories of people are not uniform because the fundamental mechanisms of stratification intersect one another, in particular sets of circumstances, to create a complex pattern of inequalities.

The studies examined give some indication of the complex inter-dependencies, though most have a primary focus on one or other dimension. Overall, they identify and describe aspects of the divisions, give some explanation of the causes and consequences of inequalities, and try to assess degrees of change. Consequently, a picture is pre-sented of privilege and deprivation, of domination and subordination, in Britain.

Reading the chapters for their substantive content thus gives detailed and authoritative appreciation of stratification in contem-porary Britain. The studies examined, however, use various methods to collect information from which to draw their conclusions. Surveys, in-depth interviews with individuals, documentary and historical research, observation, ethnography, comparison of cases, and the secondary analysis of data, are all represented. Most of the currently accepted methods of data collection are represented, each entailing different forms of research design and analysis. Probably survey methods predominate in this field, in part because of the desire to generalize about the *extent* and *pattern* of inequality, of the privileged and the deprived, the powerful and the weak. Nevertheless, the typical strengths and limitations of different methods can be appreciated by comparing the studies included. We provide examples of studies based on different methods, to make apparent how different methodologies (a topic so often discussed in a dry, technical and abstract fashion) generate different kinds of data and authorise different kinds of con-clusion. In this, a field with high political relevance, the rigorousness of the methods employed and the adequate interpretation of the data collected become a major site of controversy. The extent to which the proper handling of data, evidence and interpretation lies at the heart of a rigorous and systematic sociology should become apparent. The challenge of social research can be appreciated in a lively and grounded fashion through the fourteen studies reviewed in this book.

Alan Warde and Nick Abercrombie
Lancaster, December 1993

1

British Class Division in European Perspective

Robert Erikson and John Goldthorpe (1992), *The Constant Flux: a Study of Class Mobility in Industrial Societies*, Oxford, OUP.

Michael Savage

It is often argued that Britain is a society singularly obsessed by class. Your accent, the clothes you wear, the school you go to, the place you live, your job, and so on, can all indicate the class you come from. Visitors to other countries, for instance in North America, comment on the fact that this sort of ingrained class awareness seems less prevalent there. But is it actually true that class divisions are more rigid in Britain? Whatever people might think about class can it actually be shown that class divisions are stronger or more pervasive here?

This apparently simple question is one which sociologists should be equipped to answer. Until recently there was a remarkable lack of rigorous comparative research which allowed a satisfactory examination of this issue. Many comparative inquiries used impressionistic methods, which often ended up by reproducing the stereotypes that they were supposed to question. Or, if they did attempt more systematic analysis, they tended to measure class according to the convention used in each country. Countries use very different ways of measuring class, however, with the result that two individuals with very similar life chances, but living in different countries, might be placed in different classes, so making any results obtained unreliable and arbitary.

The Constant Flux is one of the first major research projects to confront this problem by using a common class framework to which all respondents from various national surveys are allocated. Its main aim is to examine patterns of social mobility, in order to see whether there are systematic differences in the pattern of social mobility between various countries. It thus follows a long line of social research – especially strong in Britain, with the work of Glass (1954), and Goldthorpe (1980) – which has examined the salience of social class by assessing how far people tend to stay in the same class as their parents. Indeed, *The Constant Flux* can be seen as a development and elaboration of many of the ideas developed in Goldthorpe's *Social Mobility and Class Structure in Modern Britain* (1980), which is the best known account of social mobility in Britain.

Research Design

Erikson and Goldthorpe drew upon the data gathered by various national surveys of social mobility carried out in the early 1970s. The countries examined were England, Scotland, Northern Ireland, Ireland, West Germany, France, Poland, Sweden, Hungary, Italy, the Netherlands, Czechoslavakia, USA, Japan and Australia. In each case, surveys contained information on the occupations of fathers and sons. Some also included information on women, but, apart from one chapter, the book concentrates on the nature of male social mobility. The different national surveys varied enormously in terms of sample size, from 32,109 in the case of Poland, to 1,991 for Ireland. Because the surveys differed in their adequacy, the core inquiry was restricted to England, Scotland, Northern Ireland, Ireland, West Germany, France, Poland, Hungary, and Sweden. This mix of countries allowed the authors to examine differences between capitalist and (until the 1990s) state socialist countries, between early and late industrialising countries, and also permitted examination of any differences within the British Isles, between England (and Wales), Scotland, Northern Ireland, and Ireland.

In all these countries the respondents were recoded to one of seven classes according to the nature of their job. The class schema is reproduced in *Table 1.1* p.13 (see also Reid, 1989, for a longer discussion of this class schema, although it is important to note that it is different in significant ways from that used in Goldthorpe'e earlier work, notably *Social Mobility and Class Structure in Modern Britain (1980)*, because it differentiates agricultural from industrial classes).

Fathers and sons were each allocated to one of these classes, so that it became possible to see the extent to which sons could move away from the class of their fathers. In some of their analyses Erikson and Goldthorpe divide the different national samples according to the age of respondents at the time of the survey, in order to assess how rates of mobility had changed over time. In other parts of the book the authors are more concerned to compare the findings in different countries, and they do not distinguish respondents of different ages.

Principal Findings

The Constant Flux sheds light on many issues. Here there is only room to highlight three: (i) the high rates of social mobility in all countries; (ii) (and in some ways contrary to the first point) the perpetuation of class inequalities in all European countries; and, (iii), the extent to which the British countries are typical of Europe as a whole.

(i) *The high rates of social mobility*

All industrial countries have high amounts of social mobility. *Table 1.2* p.13, shows that around two thirds of sons are in different classes to their fathers, and in some countries, especially those which have seen dramatic social and political change such as Hungary, this figure reaches a remarkable 76%. Some of this mobility however is 'short range', into classes which convey similar life chances to the class that the respondent came from. If the son of an agricultural labourer becomes an unskilled manual labour he has moved class (according to Erikson and Goldthorpe), but it is doubtful whether he is much better off. The second column of *Table 1.2* therefore indicates the amount of 'vertical' mobility, that is to say the percentage of men who moved into a class which offers either notably better or worse life chances than that which he came from. Just under half the men in most European countries are in a *significantly* different class from their fathers.

Finally, the right hand column indicates the proportions of sons moving to a higher class, or to a lower class, than their fathers. With the striking exception of Sweden, nearly all European countries have very similar amounts of upward mobility, with around one third of sons moving up the social class ladder. By any reckoning these are quite large numbers. A much smaller proportion of sons move down the social scale, and here there is considerable variation. In Poland only 8% of sons have moved down the social scale, compared with 18% in Scotland.

It may seem odd that there is more upward than downward mobility: intuitively one might expect to see similar levels of each, so that they balance each other out. The explanation for this discrepancy is that in the 20th century all industrial societies have seen the expansion of professional and managerial jobs (i.e. at the top of the class structure) and the decline of manual ones (at the bottom of the class structure). This structural change creates more 'room at the top' which is filled by people from lower social classes. It also helps to explain why there is so much more downward mobility in Scotland and England than in other European countries. It might be tempting to assume that this reflects the fact that Britain is relatively 'classless' and that the lazy or untalented sons of the privileged can more readily end up in a lower class than their fathers. In reality it is due to the fact that Britain had a large 'service class' at an earlier date than other countries, so that there were more sons who were in a position to descend the social scale.

It is not merely the case that sons are often in a different class compared to their fathers. In the course of their own lives it is also common to move between classes. Men who start their working lives in Class III (routine clerical work) are most unlikely to be in the same class later in their lives. Many will presumably have been promoted to more responsible positions. Even those starting in manual work, either as skilled workers (Class V+VI) or unskilled workers (Class VIIa) have about an even chance of moving into a different class. There

is, however, a considerable variation here between the situation in
Sweden, where just over a quarter of unskilled workers remain in this
type of work, and in the socialist countries, Hungary and Poland,
where half do. Only amongst those who begin work in the 'service class'
is there a very high chance that they stay in that class, and this is true
in all countries.

At the most basic level, it is clear that Erikson and Goldthorpe have
demonstrated that there is a considerable amount of mobility in all
European societies, regardless of their political regimes or specific
histories. But this is only half the story. The title of their book is *The
Constant Flux*. We have seen the flux – what about the constancy?

(ii) *The perpetuation of class inequality*

The figures indicated above might suggest that class is of relatively
little importance in any European country. But there are two possible
reasons why such a high degree of mobility exists. Firstly, it may
reflect the fact that societies are 'open', and that the sons of the lower
social classes can easily rise, whilst those of the lowest social class can
easily fall. Or, secondly, it may simply reflect the fact that major
occupational changes within a society force people to be mobile, and
does not indicate that a society is really 'open'. Erikson and Goldthorpe
endorse the latter view, and note two particular occupational changes
which explain high rates of mobility. The decline of agriculture has
meant that the sons of farmers and agricultural labourers have had to
move into other types of employment. The rise of professional and
managerial employment in large organizations has also created
opportunities for people from other social classes.

Erikson and Goldthorpe argue that if these types of economic
changes are taken into account, the picture is fundamentally altered.
If social mobility is thought of as the *chances* of people from one class
background, compared to those of another class background, obtaining
more rather than less desirable social class positions, then a picture of
systematic and sustained class inequality is revealed. The sons of the
service class members have much better chances of staying in the
service class than do the sons of lower social classes of moving into it.
Those from the most advantaged backgrounds are systematically more
likely to be in privileged positions themselves. This trend has changed
relatively little – if at all – throughout the 20th century.

Erikson and Goldthorpe argue that a number of factors explain
the perpetuation of class privilege. The most important of these are
concerned with inheritance. The authors distinguish three types of
inheritance factors which allow the perpetuation of class inequalities.
The first (which they label IN1) is the tendency, evident amongst all
classes, for sons to follow in the same class as their fathers, simply
because this is the easiest thing to do. Secondly, there are two types
of inheritance factors which only affect the service class and the petty
bourgoisie. These classes are usually in the best position to pass on

property to their children, which gives them extra chances of staying amongst the propertied classes. They may also pass on 'cultural capital' – the ability of middle class parents to pass on the types of cultural resources to their children which allow them to do well in formal education and hence move into jobs demanding high levels of qualifications. Both these factors are included as IN2. Thirdly, on top of both IN1 and IN2 factors, the sons of farmers are still more likely to follow in their father's footsteps. This they explain in terms of the strong cultural and social factors leading farmers to want to pass on family farms to their heirs. These three types of inheritance are the main means by which social class positions are passed on to their children.

It is difficult to convey simply the effects of these factors, since the authors develop their argument by the use of complex statistical techniques which cannot easily be explained. But, to simplify, there is a slight tendency for all sons to follow their fathers, whatever class they come from (i.e. when IN1 alone operates). This tendency becomes more pronounced amongst the sons of 'service class' members who are three and a half times more likely to be in the 'service class' themselves than would be the case if inheritance effects were not operating (i.e. when IN1 and IN2 both operate). These effects become yet more striking amongst the sons of farmers who are seven times more likely to be farmers themselves than would be the case if inheritance factors were not at work (i.e. where IN1, IN2 and IN3 factors are at work).

The discovery that inheritance is the crucial way in which class inequalities are perpetuated is of major interest. It may seem that passing on property or cultural values is only a private act between family members, but the authors show convincingly that it is the major buttress of the class system. The implications of Erikson and Goldthorpe's arguments are that the apparently high rates of mobility in industrial societies are primarily dependent on dynamic economic change rather than 'open' social structures. Although there are high rates of movement, the sons of the privileged continue to have great advantages over those in lower social classes.

(iii) *Cross-national differences*

Although Erikson and Goldthorpe argue that there is a basic similarity in social mobility processes throughout European countries, (and indeed, in all industrial countries), they are aware that there are some national specificities. *Table 1.3* p.14, indicates some of these national differences with respect to the importance of inheritance.

A positive figure indicates that the sons of the members of specific classes have a better than expected chance of being in their father's class, whilst a negative figure indicates a less than expected chance. The higher the figure, the stronger the inheritance factor at work. If the figures for IN1 are examined first, it can readily be seen that there is considerable variation. In all countries there is some sort of tendency for sons to follow fathers in all social classes, but this varies greatly between Sweden, where it is quite weak, and Ireland, where it is over three times as strong. Looking simply at the 'British' countries, it can be seen that England has the lowest propensity for sons to follow fathers, followed very closely by Northern Ireland. In Scotland, however, and especially Ireland, these factors rise substantially.

In some ways IN2 is the most important of the factors to examine, since it refers to the ability of the propertied and cultured classes, the 'service class' and small property owners, to pass on their advantages to their sons. The most remarkable finding here is that IN2 is actually slightly weaker in England than in Europe as a whole, and it is strongest of all in Poland, which, as a state socialist country formally committed to equality, might have been expected to see low values here. All the 'British' countries have roughly similar profiles, though Scotland comes out as the country with the highest values.

Finally, IN3 refers to the ability of farmers to pass on their position to their sons. Here the values fluctuate widely. In Poland the figures are negative, indicating that the sons of farmers actually have less chance of being farmers themselves than the sons of other classes. In West Germany however, the values are exceptionally high. The figures for the 'British' countries fall generally in the middle, close to the average for European countries, though the figures for Northern Ireland are quite high.

The general conclusion reached by Erikson and Goldthorpe is that, far from England being exceptional in the strength of its class divisions, it is actually rather average. The authors see England and France as having the 'most central' patterns of social mobility, which they argue is due to the fact that they have both industrialised in a relatively 'unforced' way. Scotland, however, is in important respects different from England, in a way which would seriously invalidate claims about there being a 'British' class structure. The concentration of industrial employment in central Scotland, centred around Glasgow and Edinburgh, has reduced mobility chances between urban and rural populations, and caused more class immobility than in England. Northern Ireland, by contrast, is much closer to England. Finally, Ireland has emerged as one of the most closed societies in Europe, with very low levels of social mobility. For instance, *Table 1.2* shows that is more unusual for 'service class' members in Ireland to experience downward mobility in the course of their careers than in any other European country.

The general conclusion reached by the authors is that structural inequalities in mobility chances are inevitable in all industrial capitalist societies, but that they can be modified by particular factors operating in each country. There is no doubting which country Erikson and Goldthorpe regard as being the most open – Sweden. The democratic socialist policies pursued over long periods by the Swedish Social Democrats are seen as offering the best chance of reducing – though not ending – class inequalities.

Critical Observations

The approach to social mobility developed by Goldthorpe in this book, and in his earlier work, has been the subject of much criticism and debate. One line of attack by sociologists such as Peter Saunders (1990) has been to suggest that he is concerned to downplay the real extent of mobility, preferring to emphasise class inequalities in mobility chances (see the discussion in Payne, 1992). But, as the discussion above has indicated, this is an unfair criticism. Erikson and Goldthorpe are well aware that there are high rates of social mobility in industrial societies, but the vital question which they pursue is how systematic class advantages can be sustained in the face of such apparently high rates of mobility.

A more serious problem with *The Constant Flux*, is its handling of gender issues (see the general discussion in Marshall *et al.*, 1988). The book focuses on men, and only considers women's social mobility in one chapter. Here the authors justify their exclusion of women by noting that, since women are subordinated to men in the family, it makes sense to examine the social mobility of men only for this is the key way by which households are 'attached' to the class structure. They also argue that even if women's mobility is studied, the patterns it shows are little different from those of men. The authors, are, however still open to criticism. They have nothing to say about how patterns of divorce or separation problematize any attempt to link a woman's position to that of a male partner for her entire life. Furthermore, increasing numbers of households contain women in higher social class jobs then men. In fact, Erikson and Goldthorpe do admit significant modifications to their analysis when these factors are taken into account.

The authors also have nothing to say on ethnicity and social mobility, even though it is commonly argued that many industrial countries have recruited a substantial group of immigrant labourers or 'guest workers' to perform the worst paid jobs at the bottom of the class structure. This might allow native workers relatively high mobility chances at their expense. Nowhere in the book, however, is this idea discussed or examined.

Erikson and Goldthorpe have also been criticized for stressing inter-generational mobility rather than work-life mobility (Sorenson, 1986). Inter-generational mobility refers to the extent to which a parent's class at one period in his or her life is different from a child's class at one point in his or her life. Critics such as Sorenson claim that this is misleading because it 'freezes' a person's class position arbitrarily at one point in their life, with the result that the mobility tables produced are unrepresentative, because they ignore the frequently high degree of mobility experienced by both parent and child over their lifetimes. Erikson and Goldthorpe do recongise that there are problems with the use of inter-generational mobility tables, and they show that there is much more national variation in patterns of work-life mobility than in inter-generational mobility. They do, however, counter with a strong point. If Sorenson is correct in arguing that inter-generational mobility tables are arbitary, one would not expect to find the regularity of patterns which are in fact found.

Finally, Erikson and Goldthorpe's analyses depend, ultimately, on the adequacy of the class schema used. The authors play up the pragmatism of their schema. They claim that there is no point making theoretical distinctions about class if these cannot be empirically put into use. A good example of this is the author's use of the 'service class', which encompasses a great variety of types – from aristocrats, managing directors, MPs, senior professionals, to junior managers and teachers. Since there are only very small numbers of these in the population they cannot be adequately distinguished in sample surveys, and so it makes pragmatic sense to include them all in 'the service class'. The danger is that their account of class becomes divorced from theoretical analyses of class which might explain the reasons for class inequality.

Conclusion

The Constant Flux will undoubtedly become the standard point of departure for anyone interested in class divisions in comparative perspective. It does have serious problems, especially in regard to its treatment of gender and ethnicity, but debate will probably be couched in terms of considering how a more satisfactory account of these will alter the findings and arguments produced here. Erikson and Goldthorpe have produced a rigorous framework for the examination of social mobility which allows patterns of both commonality and variation to be given due weight, and this is an impressive achievement.

Bibliography

Glass, D.V. (1954), *Social Mobility In Britain*, London, Routledge and Kegan Paul.
Goldthorpe, J.H. with Llewellyn, C. and Payne, G. (1980), *Social Mobility and Class Structure in Modern Britain*, Oxford, Clarendon.
Marshall, G., Newby, H., Rose, D., Vogler, C. (1988), *Social Class in Modern Britain*, London, Unwin Hyman.
Payne, G. (1992), 'Competing Views of Contemporary Social Mobility and Social Divisions', in R. Burrows and C. Marsh (eds.), *Consumption and Class: divisions and change*, Basingstoke, Macmillan.
Reid, I. (1989), *Social Class Differences in Modern Britain*, (3rd ed.), London, Fontana.
Saunders, P. (1990), *Social Class and Stratification*, London, Tavistock.
Sorenson, A.B. (1986), 'Theory and Methodology in Stratification Research', in U. Himmelstrand (ed.), *The Sociology of Structure and Action: Vol 1, Sociology from crisis to science?*, London, Sage.

Appendices

Table 1.1 The Erikson-Goldthorpe Class Schema

I + II	– Service Class	(professionals, administrators and managers, higher grade technicians, supervisors of non-manual workers)
III	– Routine non-manual workers	(routine non-manual employees in administration and commerce, sales personnel, other rank and file service workers)
IVa + b	– Petty Bourgoisie	(small proprietors and artisans etc., with and without employees)
IVc	– Farmers	(farmers and smallholders and other self-employed workers in primary production)
V + VI	– Skilled Workers	(lower grade technicians, supervisors of manual workers, skilled manual workers)
VIIa	– Non-skilled workers	(semi- and unskilled manual workers)
VIIb	– Agricultural labourers	

Notes: The numbers refer to the older Goldthorpe class schema, which is discussed in I. Reid, *Social Class Differences in Britain*, (3rd ed.), pp.70–71

Table 1.2 Decomposition of total mobility rates (TMR) into total vertical (TV) and total non-vertical (TNV) mobility and of total vertical mobility into total upward (TU) and total downward (TD) mobility

Nation	TMR	TV	TNV	TV/TNV	TU	TD	TU/TD
ENG	65	50	15	3.4	32	17	1.9
FRA	65	44	21	2.1	32	12	2.5
FRG	62	47	15	3.2	33	14	2.4
HUN	76	45	32	1.4	35	9	3.8
IRL	58	39	19	2.1	30	9	3.4
NIR	63	45	18	2.5	34	11	3.0
POL	60	43	16	2.7	35	8	4.5
SCO	64	51	13	3.9	33	18	1.8
SWE	73	54	19	2.9	42	13	3.3

(Erikson and Goldthorpe, 1992, Table 6.3)

Table 1.3 Effect parameters of accepted models*

Nation	IN1	IN2	IN3
ENG	0.47	0.71	0.77
FRA	0.41	0.92	1.00
FRG	0.49	*1.17*	2.17
HUN	0.50	ns	*1.01*
IRL	0.90	0.68	0.80
NIR	0.48	0.72	1.45
POL	0.75	1.23	−0.37
SCO	*0.63*	0.90	0.83
SWE	0.28	0.65	0.78
CORE	0.43	0.81	0.96

Note:
  * Parameters directly affected by modifications to the core model are in italic type; instances where a parameter initially returned a non-significant value at the 5 per cent level and has then been omitted in re-estimating the model are indicated by ns.
(ibid., Table 5.3)

2

Middle Class Formation

Mike Savage, James Barlow, Peter Dickens and Tony Fielding (1992), *Property, Bureaucracy, and Culture; Middle Class Formation in Contemporary Britain*, London, Routledge.

Nicholas Abercrombie

Introduction

Sociologists have long been interested in the middle class. Debate has focused on its size, where its boundaries should be drawn, its growth and consequent social and political importance, and the degree to which it is, in reality, made up of fragments which cannot be unified. This last issue has taken up most attention. The prevailing assumption is that the middle class is made up of several parts, two of which are of particular importance. The first of these comprises routine white-collar workers – clerks, secretaries, shop assistants – many of whom have pay and conditions not dissimilar to those of manual workers. The second group, sometimes referred to as the service class, is made up of professional and managerial workers who seem to have market and work situations very much superior to the routine white-collar workers.

The service class is the subject of this study, which takes as its starting point the propositions that this section of the middle class is important, is changing rapidly, and no longer conforms to the sociological stereotypes held of it.

Principal findings

(i) *Class theory*

Savage *et al.*'s book is based on a particular view of how classes are constituted. For them, social classes are social collectivities – 'groups of people with shared levels of income and remuneration, lifestyles, cultures, political orientations and so forth' (Savage *et al.*, 1992, p.5). They are also a particular *kind* of collectivity, being organized around relations of exploitation where 'one person's welfare is obtained at the expense of another' (ibid., p.6). In order to be able to exploit others, a social class has to have assets of some kind. Critical to the capacity to exploit others is the manner in which assets can be *stored*. Assets which can be stored, especially if they can be passed on from generation to generation, are the most effective bases for the exploitation of others. In the case of the service class, there are three kinds of asset – property, organization and culture. Property assets give the most effective basis for class formation since they can be readily stored as capital. Organizational assets are those that derive from a superior position in an organization. Managers, for example, are able to expoit the labour of others. However, unlike property, organizational assets cannot readily be passed on to others and this lack of storage capacity makes them relatively weak. Cultural assets refer to those qualities of taste, opinion, belief, knowledge, skill that have become defined by society (or by dominant social groups) as being superior. Cultural assets are comparitively easy to store and to pass on. Their drawback is that they do not readily lend themselves to the exploitation of others. The only way that they can do so is to be used to acquire other assets. For example, cultural assets can be used to gain educational qualifications which, in turn, allow the possessor to get superior jobs in organizations.

Although the possession of assets is the foundation of a social class, it does not determine its *formation*. Assets provide the basis, but other factors determine how a class is formed as an entity, how unified it is, and, above all, how it *acts* as a class. The question is how people draw upon assets to form classes. A large number of factors can determine class formation. In the case of the middle class for Savage *et al.*, the important factors are intervention by the state, gender relations, and social and spatial mobility.

Class formation is thus a contingent question; possession or non-possession of assets does not necessarily create a social class, it just makes it possible. For example, the fact that the middle class is based on three different types of asset might lead to a fragmentation into three different classes or it might, under certain circumstances, lead to a unified class.

(ii) *Class assets*

(a) *organizational assets*
In considering how classes are formed in modern Britain, Savage *et al.*'s first task is to see how class assets have been altered. Their argument is that organizational assets are of declining importance. The greater insecurity of organizational assets is produced by changes in the structure of companies. These are now less bureaucratic and much less reliant on organizational hierarchies in which managers have clear positions of authority. At the same time, companies have increasingly come to need the skills and knowledge of professionally trained people who can move about between companies. The net result of these

changes is that there is less of an internal labour market in many companies (see *Table 2.1* p.23). Managers cannot rely on staying with the
same company for life by capitalizing on the assets given by a position
in a bureaucracy. Consequently, managers try to convert organizational assets into other forms. For example, they may seek property
assets by becoming entrepreneurs or cultural assets by acquiring
professional qualifications.

The position of professional workers, on the other hand, has been
enhanced. Traditionally reliant on cultural assets, these groups have
more recently been in demand in companies for their professional
skills. The result is that they have been able to acquire organizational
assets as well. At the same time professional workers have continued
to find employment in the state sector. Savage *et al.* argue that, appear-
ances to the contrary, the position of professionals in public service has
not been harmed by recent attempts to reduce the size of the sector.
This is particularly so since the introduction of managerial hierarchies
into the public services has typically resulted in those hierarchies
being staffed by professionals; in this area too, professionals are able
to turn their cultural assets derived from a professional training into
organizational assets.

(b) property assets

One of the most important changes in Britain in recent years has been
the growth of owner-occupancy of housing. Savage *et al.*, argue that
this gain in property assets has had a role in middle class formation.
Since 1945 the extent of owner-occupancy has increased from about
30% of the housing stock to about 67% by the late 1980s. While this
has certainly brought many working-class people into owner-
occupancy, nearly all middle-class households are now home owners.
Middle-class households, furthermore, make disproportionate gains
from house ownership. Since the second world war, the price of housing
has increased dramatically, even allowing for inflation, creating the
possibility of capital gain when a house is sold. The longer history of
the middle class in owner-occupation has meant that the potential gain
that they have accrued is much greater than that gained by the
working class. In addition, there is some evidence that they pay less
for it as employers subsidize the housing costs of some middle-class
employees. Although at the moment the inheritance of wealth as the
result of house ownership is not particularly significant, the middle
class again will gain disproportionately since their parents have been
owner occupiers that much longer.

Even if the middle class has benefited greatly from investment in
housing, it is a separate question whether or not they set out deliberately to make these gains. Savage *et al.* conclude from the evidence that
middle-class households do not pursue a *career* of trying to maximize
gains from housing by, for example, moving often. Nonetheless, there
is evidence that some households are realizing the money locked up in
their houses, either by further borrowing against the security of the

property or by trading down, and are using that money to start businesses.

(c) cultural assets

Savage *et al.*'s arguments about the role of cultural assets in middle-class formation is partly drawn from the work of Bourdieu (1984). Bourdieu's focus is on the interplay between cultural and economic capital and his main argument is that people actively invest cultural capital to realize economic capital and *vice-versa*. The complex relationship between economic and cultural capital gives rise to a number of competing groups within the middle class. Bourdieu distinguishes three such groups. A dominant group, senior industrial managers for example, has a great deal of economic capital but relatively little cultural capital. Second, there is a group of people in the rapidly growing group of occupations such as the media, the helping professions, and marketing. These have a great deal of cultural capital. Lastly, there is a group low in economic but high in cultural capital – teachers and artists, for example. For Bourdieu, these groups, and others, are engaged in a constant struggle with one another to further their social position, using and enhancing their possession of the different types of capital.

Savage *et al.* develop Bourdieu's position with an analysis of the British Market Research Bureau's Target Group Index. As a result of their analysis, Savage *et al.* distinguish three groups, each of which has very distinctive cultural tastes, within the middle class. Their conclusions differ from those of Bourdieu largely because they argue that he neglects the crucial significance of those employed in organizations, who are dependent on organizational assets.

The Target Group Index survey indicates the existence of three major middle-class lifestyle groupings each with a distinct social base. An ascetic style concentrates on healthy pastimes, including exercise and sport, combined with an interest in high culture pursuits, such as visiting art galleries and going to concerts. People with this cultural orientation tend to be recruited from public sector professionals. Managers and public sector bureaucrats, on the other hand, have an undistinctive culture; there are no pastimes or pursuits that particularly mark them out. The postmodern lifestyle is adopted by private sector professionals and specialists. The postmodern culture is apparently paradoxical in that it combines an interest in health, exercise, sport and fitness, with a dedication to high living as manifested in champagne drinking and foreign eating styles. In the postmodern lifestyle, the traditional boundaries and distinctions between cultural pursuits have broken down. The postmodern style is gaining influence, partly as a result of the growing importance of the private sector professionals and specialists described earlier. Savage *et al.* note that the adoption of lifestyles is also interwoven with gender, age and regional factors. A young, male, London-based advertising executive, for example, is particularly likely to adopt a postmodern lifestyle.

(iii) *Class formation and action*

A description of class assets does not tell one how classes are actually formed; groups based on different kinds of asset can be united into a coherent class or they can be prised apart. Historically, Savage *et al.* argue that the three types of asset have given rise to three distinct social classes with the distinction between the professions on the one hand and the managerial and propertied sectors on the other being particularly marked. In contemporary society a variety of processes affect the relationship between the three sectors.

(a) social mobility
One of the most important features affecting class formation is social mobility. If the social origins of members of the middle class are diverse, then the class is less likely to *act* as a class. If, on the other hand, the class is self-recruiting, children following parents in being members of the class, then it is more likely to act as a class. Savage *et al.*'s argument is based on an analysis of the census and of the British General Election Survey (see the section on Methodology below). Their conclusions are that the mobility experience of different members of the middle class is related to the possession of different assets.

Considering first career mobility – the way that people stay in their career throughout their lives – there turn out to be three different types of mobility within the middle class. Professionals tend to be a stable, self-enclosed group with considerable security. They have a good chance of maintaining their professional position for all of their lives whereas other middle class people, managers for example, have a relatively poor chance of becoming professionals. Managers, on the other hand, are a fairly open group. They recruit from other middle class groupings and a relatively high proportion of them are downwardly mobile. The self-employed middle class appears to have a stable core but it is less closed than the professional grouping, recruiting a high proportion of its members from those with a managerial background.

Another way to look at the impact of social mobility on class formation is to analyze mobility, not over a career, but between generations. In their analysis of this issue, the authors use the British General Election Survey which allows them to plot intergenerational movements between managerial, professional and self-employed groups. As Savage *et al.* expected, the professional grouping emerge as the most closed. Over one-third of professionals' children move into professional work themselves, while only 19% of managers' children become managers and only 15% of the self-employed become self-employed. The conclusion drawn is that cultural assets are more easily transfered across generations than either organizational or property assets.

Even more important than this finding, however, is the discovery that very large numbers of *managers'* children become *professionals*. More children of managers become professionals (23%) than become managers (19%). What appears to be happening here, therefore, is that the *organizational* assets of manager parents are being traded in for the *cultural* assets for their children.

The educational system is the means by which this trade is managed. It seems as if the school system in effect disseminates cultural assets throughout the population and, in particular to the children of managers. However, Savage *et al.* argue that the comprehensive school system, by its methods of selection, actually favours the children of professional classes, those with already high cultural assets. They compare the educational attainments of professionals' and managers' children in different age groups. While professionals have always been at an advantage in the attainment of qualifications, the gap between professionals and mangers has widened as the school system has become comprehensive. For example, in the youngest age group examined, most of whom were educated in a comprehensive system, one-third of professionals' children got degrees, compared with only one-sixth of managers' children. The result of these changes, in the long-run, is likely to be that the middle class will become more frag- mented, not more unified, by the education system and the professional groupings will become more self-recruiting. The potential fragmenta- tion of the middle class is likely to be further promoted by a greater diversity of household types. The process of middle class formation will increasingly depend not simply on the assets on which an individual can draw, but on the assets on which a *household* can draw. There is no longer a typical middle class household, but a wide variation in household types and therefore in household incomes.

(b) spatial mobility
Spatial mobility is important in class formation because a class is more likely to acquire an identity if its members remain in the same area for a length of time. In popular mythology the South East functions as an area of this kind because it is thought to contain a large number of middle class occupations. Savage *et al.* agree that the South East is indeed middle class in the sense that 'control' functions – those of research, planning, financing, and marketing, for example – tend to be concentrated there. However, the concentration of middle class occupa- tions does not necessarily indicate the *formation* of a middle class.

It is crucial how these occupational positions are filled. Thus middle class positions might be filled locally by people moving from working class jobs or they might be filled by people moving into the area from other middle class occupations. The character of class formation will be dfferent in these two cases.

The South East has a distinctive role in middle class formation. It has a high degree of fluidity between different sectors of the middle class – professionals becoming managers or managers becoming self- employed, for example. It also is an area where a relatively high proportion of the working class go into middle class occupations. Those people already established in middle class positions are not, on the other hand, attracted to the region and, indeed, leave it to go elsewhere. The South East functions as a kind of 'escalator' region or a machine for upward mobility. First, it attracts young recruits to the middle class directly from the education system. Second, it promotes these young people, together with its own, very rapidly into senior positions. Third, it sends out to the provinces the now established middle class as their career begins to mature.

(c) Politics
A fundamental aspect of class formation concerns the political orientations of members of a class. Formation of a class will be helped by a common political orientation, of which voting behaviour is a good index. Analysis of the British General Election Survey indicates that there are differences within the middle class between professional and managerial groups. The former are distinctive in the support they give to the Liberal Democrats and they are also more likely to vote Labour. Interestingly this difference is even more pronounced when social mobility is taken into account. The children of managers who are also managers themselves are very likely to vote Conservative (74% do so). The professional children of professional parents, on the other hand, are unlikely to vote Conservative (only 39% do so). Indeed, they are somewhat less likely to vote conservative than the electorate as a whole.

Savage *et al.* attribute this difference between professionals and managers to the relationship to the state. Professionals employed by the state are less likely to vote Conservative than their counterparts in private industry. But it is not just the state's role as employer that is relevent, for private sector professionals are less likely to vote Conservative than managers in that sector. It is the role of the state in education that is crucial for it makes effective the cultural assets that professionals depend upon. Professionals, therefore, have an interest in maintaining and extending the role of the state.

Methodology

Property, Bureaucracy and Culture is a study that depends on the analysis of secondary data – that is, data gathered by someone else for a different purpose. Further than that, it actually comprises a number of studies based on different data sources. Three are particularly important. The Longitudinal Study of the British Census links together the census records of 1% of the English and Welsh population between 1971 and 1981. This provides very large numbers for analysis with over half a million people in the sample and some 34,000 individuals in the service class. Savage *et al.* use this data source for their fine-grained analysis of career mobility between 1971 and 1981 and of spatial mobility between the English regions.

The British Market Research Bureau's Target Group Index (TGI) is used by Savage *et al.* for an analysis of the lifestyle and consumption habits of the middle class. This is an annual survey of 24,000 adults, with respondents asked to provide details of their consumption habits. The survey allows very precise descriptions of life-styles. Thus groups can be distinguished by whether or not they drink brandy, take holidays in foreign cities, or eat in French restaurants. (See *Table 2.2* p.24). Some of the difficulties inherent in secondary analysis are illustrated by the use of this data source since the social class categories used by the TGI are not identical to those employed by Savage *et al*. This is partly overcome by the fact that TGI conduct a separate study of the middle class groupings with 5,500 individuals which enables analysis at the level of individual occupations.

The third major data source is the British General Election Survey of 1987 which is used, because it inquires about father's occupation, for analysis both of voting and of social mobility. Its drawback is that it uses a relatively small sample of 3,500 people which does not permit analysis at a very detailed level.

Evaluation

Savage *et al*.'s study represents a welcome move away from a view of the class structure based simply on relatively static occupational classifications towards a dynamic theory founded on assets which are realizable in particular circumstances. At the same time, the study uses some of the assumptions of the occupational schemes without making it clear how they work. For example, for Savage *et al*., class has something to do with exploitation and the point of the various assets is that they enable the exploitation of the labour of others. Although it may be relatively easy to see how this might work with property assets (although perhaps not for self-employment), it is not so clear for organizational assets. In other words, the theory of exploitation is not spelled out. To some extent this omission is related to another line of criticism. The middle class seems to exist in a kind of vacuum unaffected by the existence of other classes (see Carter, 1993). However, the formation of the middle class must be crucially affected by the formation and actions of the working class and the upper class. These are classes with assets realizable in particular circumstances and whose struggles must be one of the factors affecting middle class formation. It is likely that the upper class depends on property assets, for example, but it is not clear how the mobilization of these affect the middle class and, in particular, how they will affect the exploitation of *middle class labour* by the upper class.

One of the drawbacks of class theories based on occupational categories is that they create boundary problems. They automatically create such problems as: are shop workers middle class or working class? One of the advantages of Savage *et al*.'s scheme is that these problems become less severe. Classes are formed by a variety of processes which can change over time with the result that class boundaries can alter. This does, however, have the drawback that there is a certain contingency built into the scheme. The factors that influence class formation seem to constitute an almost random list. There is no theoretical reason why some factors are included and others are not.

One of the great contributions of *Property, Bureaucracy and Culture* is the emphasis on culture as a class asset. It seems entirely plausible to see education as such an asset, in that it leads to middle class occupations, and the analysis of the way that managers transform their organizational positions into professional ones is one of the most interesting features of the argument. However, it is less clear how the life-style features of culture constitute an asset. Of necessity, cultural tastes and pursuits such as going to the opera or brandy drinking only constitute an asset if they are *recognized* by others in the class (and in other classes) as doing so. There is no evidence presented that they do so. The difficulty here is rather similar to that presented by the concept of status used by the older occupational schemes (see Lockwood, 1993). Status used to be seen, not as a determinant of class formation but rather one of its consequences. Similarly, Savage *et al.* need to do more work to show how culture actively functions as an *asset*, independently of education, recognized by others.

Conclusion

Savage *et al.* argue that the middle class as a whole is founded on the possession of three kinds of asset – organizational, property, and cultural. The question that they set themselves is whether the class can be unified or whether it will fragment into three groupings each of which is based on a different asset. Historically, there has been such a fragmentation, especially between the professional and managerial groupings. In contemporary society, although there may be forces that are making for unification, Savage *et al.* conclude that the fragmentation persists.

Bibliography

Bourdieu, P. (1984), *Distinction*, London, Routledge.

Carter, B. (1993), Review of 'Property, Bureaucracy and Culture' in *Sociology*, Vol. 27, No. 2.

Lockwood, D. (1993), Review of 'Property, Bureaucracy and Culture' in *Work, Employment and Society*, Vol. 7, No. 3.

Appendices

Table 2.1 Percentage of workers in internal labour markets in financial services

	Banks		Building Societies		Insurance	
	1978	1985	1978	1985	1978	1985
Career clerical	61	41	45	30	62	56
Non-career clerical	30	40	49	55	25	26
Specialists	2	8	1	5	7	11
Managers	7	11	5	10	6	7

(Savage *et al.*, 1992, Table 4.1)

Table 2.2 Consumption by managers and professionals 1987–88. Uses AB Survey as a base. Vertical axis = Target Group Index (TGI) where the value for Great Britain = 100. Brackets are used when cell counts are too low to produce reliable data.

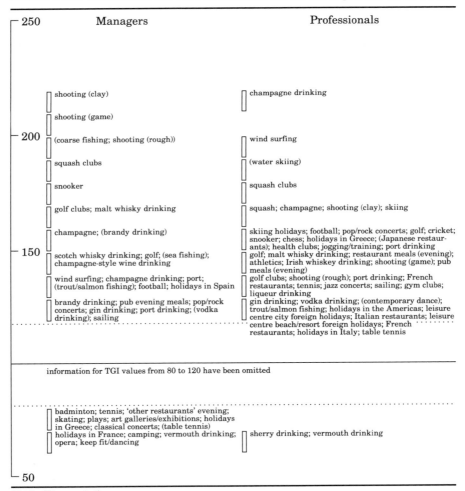

(ibid., Figure 6.4)

3

Class and Class Consciousness

G. Marshall, D. Rose, H. Newby and C. Vogler (1988), *Social Class in Modern Britain*, London, Unwin Hyman.

Paul Bagguley

Class is one of the central concepts of sociology. Much of the research carried out by sociologists in Britain between the 1950s and 1970s was centrally concerned with class. A person's class position has been used to explain differences of culture, politics and health. More specifically, one of the main themes of the British sociology of class has been the changing nature of the working class and the class basis of politics.

Social Class in Modern Britain is the definitive study of class and the class basis of politics in contemporary Britain. The aim of the study is to examine the declining significance of class in British social and political life. The authors use data from a national survey to consider a wide range of issues in class analysis including: How should sociologists conceptualise and measure social class? How have class processes, such as social mobility, changed recently in Britain? To what extent is class still an important source of social identity and basis for political action in Britain?

Research Design

The study was based on structured interviews with a national sample of 1770 men and women. This sample was obtained from addresses on the electoral register selected in three stages. Firstly, 100 parliamentary constituencies were selected, after being stratified according to their social characteristics, such as the percentage of people owning their own houses.

Secondly, in each constituency two polling districts were selected in a similar way. Finally, 19 addresses in each polling district were selected at random. It was not a simple random sample, but a *multistage stratified random sample*, which goes to show how complex survey research is becoming before any questions are even asked!

Over 130 questions were asked in each interview by the professional interviewers of a private research company. The questions covered a range of issues about people's economic position, and their political attitudes (see *Appendix B*, p.35). Most importantly they asked questions which enabled the authors to create a variety of models of the class structure (see *Tables 3.1, 3.2, 3.3*, pp.32–34).

Principal Findings

Marshall *et al.*, consider several important themes: social mobility, proletarianization, class identity and voting.

(i) *Social mobility*

On social mobility their results broadly support those of the Nuffield studies (see Goldthorpe, 1987). Whilst absolute social mobility had increased – there is more upward mobility – relative social mobility had not changed. By absolute social mobility sociologists mean the overall pattern of movements between class positions, or the total amount of mobility. In contrast, relative social mobility refers to the comparative chances of social mobility for people from different backgrounds (see Haralambos, 1990, p.104). In these terms Goldthorpe had found that the chances of someone from the middle class staying in the middle class were much greater than someone from the working class entering the middle class. Absolute social mobility had increased only because of the expansion of middle class places in the class structure, but relative social mobility remained much the same.

Marshall *et al.* challenge Goldthorpe's conventional view of class analysis, which suggests that sociologists should only consider men's mobility. They show that, whilst men's and women's relative mobility chances are the same, men's absolute mobility chances are much better than women's. Women are at a disadvantage in terms of inter-generational mobility and in their own careers. Men are more likely to enter *both* the service class *and* the working class than women. However, women are more likely to enter the intermediate class of routine white-collar workers than men. Whatever their class origins, most women enter the intermediate class when they start employment (see *Table 3.4*, p.35).

(ii) *Proletarianization*

Marshall *et al.* distinguish four types of proletarianization discussed by sociologists. Firstly, some, such as Wright, have argued that the working class is growing in size, so the class structure as a whole is being proletarianized. Secondly, for Goldthorpe, the crucial issue is whether *individuals* are being proletarianized due to downward social mobility. Thirdly, for sociologists such as Crompton, the question is whether or not *types of job*, such as clerical work are being proletarianized. Finally, there is the question of socio-political proletarianization, that is, the extent to which people identify themselves with the working class and its political interests.

They conclude that the size of the working class is declining – refuting Wright. People, furthermore, tend not to be downwardly mobile, refuting that model of proletarianization. Marshall *et al.*'s data also contradict Stanworth's feminist claims that women are downwardly mobile. They found that women's relative mobility is the same as that of men.

They consider the proletarianization of clerical jobs by asking not only whether or not people felt that their jobs had been deskilled, but also questions about what people did in their jobs. Their results, they argue, justify placing clerical workers in an intermediate class category. Clerks are not deskilled like many manual workers, but they do not have the autonomy and control at work that is reported by many professionals and managers. In terms of measures of socio-political proletarianization, such as class identity and union membership, clerical workers are more like the middle class than manual workers. This suggests, according to Marshall *et al.*, that it is legitimate to consider them an intermediate class that has not been proletarianized in any sense.

(iii) *Class identity and class consciousness*

The authors also assess whether or not class is still a source of social identity and political conflict in Britain. At the time of their study, in the mid-1980s, there appeared to be a convincing case for the reduced salience of class in British society. Changes in the economy were transforming the class structure. The growth of service industries and the decline of manufacturing meant that traditional male manual working class factory jobs were disappearing. Simultaneously, professional, managerial and administrative jobs had grown in number. So the traditional working class was shrinking and the new middle class or service class was growing.

It was thought during the 1980s that people no longer had a strong attachment to class identity, with, for example, fewer working class people voting Labour. People were engaging in 'privatized consumption', i.e. people were aspiring to buy homes and fill them with consumers goods. The working class had become divided between affluent home owners voting Conservative, and the poor trapped in council estates and voting Labour. Not only had the working class declined in size, but it had lost its traditional solidarity and patterns of community life. There appeared to be new, and increasingly significant, divisions *within* the working class.

Marshall *et al.* summarise their conclusions here in terms of *instrumental collectivism*. This means that people join and support working class organizations, such as trade unions, for instrumental reasons of self-interest. These instrumental reasons are to do with their own economic well-being. In other words, people join unions to obtain pay rises and to give them security in their jobs.

Marshall *et al.* argue most people perceive the distribution of income and wealth in Britain as both unequal and unfair. Many believe that this situation *could* be changed towards a more equitable order without radically transforming capitalism. However, respondents are cynical and fatalistic about the ability and commitment of politicians to effect such changes. This they describe as *informed fatalism*. Informed fatalism involves a recognition of class inequality. This recognition is what Marshall *et al.* call the *cognitive sphere* of people's attitudes. In addition, this informed fatalism involves a belief in the impossibility of change. This is what Marshall *et al.* refer to as the evaluative sphere of people's attitudes; how people judge what is desirable or possible. Informed fatalists are pragmatic, putting up with the present situation, and supporting organizations such as trade unions for their own personal instrumental reasons, such as pay rises. Social order in British society thus does not depend on shared values and beliefs, but upon the fatalism of the lower classes:

> We find that class is still the most common source of social identity and retains its salience as such. It is true that the collectivism of our respondents can most appropriately be characterised as instrumental. To that extent it reflects the pursuit of self-interest rather than collective improvement. However, our data also suggest that such instrumentalism is an entirely pragmatic response to a distributional order and distributional mechanisms that are perceived to be unjust, but are accepted as largely unalterable facts of life. This general perspective may be summarized as one of 'realism', 'resignation', 'cynicism', or – as we would prefer to describe it – 'informed fatalism'. Its origins lie in the evaluative rather than the cognitive sphere. People are often aware of alternatives but they are, on the whole, resigned to the fact that they can do little or nothing to help achieve these. Our findings suggest, then, that contemporary British society lacks a moral order, and that its cohesion is rooted more in resignation and routine than consensus and approval. (Marshall *et al.*, 1988, p.143)

Class was the most accessible source of identity for most people in their survey, but this made little impact on their individual capacities for class action, as people believed that such action would be ineffectual. Furthermore, Marshall *et al.*, found that people held complex and contradictory views about society. With so little ideological consistency, they show that there are no clear class ideologies among the population at large. They argue that only class based organizations such as political parties and trade unions develop coherent class ideologies. However, they believe that this does not mean that class is entirely irrelevant to individual attitudes and behaviour.

The authors maintain that class position remains the most important social structural factor shaping people's attitudes. Class position was better than employment sector, housing tenure, welfare dependency, sex, income or education in explaining people's sympathy for working class views of society. Furthermore, there were no age differences in class consciousness, and this, they argue, shows that class consciousness is not declining over time.

According to Marshall *et al.*, divisions within the working class have been well established since the nineteenth century. Similarly, the instrumental collectivism of the contemporary working class was widespread over a hundred years ago, when people joined trade unions to obtain wage increases. In short, little has changed in their view.

(iv) *Class and voting behaviour*

The main point of reference for Marshall *et al.*'s discussion of class and politics – voting behaviour – is the debate around the class dealignment thesis. This was developed most thoroughly by Ivor Crewe, who argued that classes are becoming less and less attached to their 'natural' class parties. Fewer middle class people are voting Conservative and fewer working class people are voting Labour.

They argue that the class dealignment thesis is wrong. It is not the case that the working class is deserting Labour. In relative terms the working class still votes disproportionately for the Labour Party and the middle class still votes disproportionately for the Conservatives. What explains Labour's electoral weakness, according to Marshall *et al.*, is their loss of votes across all social classes, in addition to the decline in the overall size of the working class. Divisions within the working class, such as housing tenure, have only a limited effect. Council house tenants only appear to vote disproportionately for the Labour Party because most of them are working class. Similarly the sector of employment has a limited effect on the relationship between class and voting. Its only real impact is on the service class, where those employed in the public sector, such as teachers, doctors, nurses, etc., are more likely to vote Labour. So the authors conclude that class is still the most important factor shaping people's voting behaviour.

Critical Observations

Class analysis is declining in popularity among sociologists, especially when class is used to explain behaviour such as voting. Surprisingly, there have been few outright rejections of Marshall *et al.*'s analysis to suggest that their theoretical conclusions are largely wrong. Critical discussions have focused on methodological questions and the issue of class identity.

The strongest objections have come from Peter Saunders (1989, 1990). From a broadly 'new right' position he argues that Marshall *et al.*'s research reflects the dominant left-wing bias in British sociology, what he calls socialist-egalitarian values. Throughout the study, from the questions they initially chose to ask (see *Appendix B*, p.35 for examples) to their conclusions, Saunders argues, Marshall *et al.* assume that class inequalities do exist and, thus, they merely judge between one kind of class analysis and another.

Two aspects of Marshall *et al.*'s work attract detailed criticism from Saunders. Firstly, he argues that they ignore the growth of *absolute* social mobility, and focus too much of their attention on *relative* social mobility. He argues that the very concept of relative social mobility – the comparative chance of an individual's shifting from their class of origin – reflects a left-wing bias. As used by Marshall *et al.*, it has two problems in Saunders view:

> The first is its assumption that the only change worth talking about is one where top dogs lose, rather than where everyone gains. The second is its assumption that everybody is equally capable of rising to fill the top positions in society. (Saunders, 1990, p.81)

For Saunders, the authors of *Social Class in Modern Britain* have ignored the benefits of free market capitalism. He believes these benefits to be widespread, as reflected in increased rates of *absolute* mobility. Marshall *et al.* tend to emphasise the continuity in the *relative* rates. Saunders accepts that people are not equally capable of reaching the top of the class structure, but maintains that the concept of relative social mobility automatically entails this assumption.

The second main criticism from Saunders concerns the design of Marshall *et al.*'s questionnaire. He believes that their questions were ordered in a way that produced results biased towards their own views. In particular, he points but that they asked several questions about class *before* asking people if they thought that they belonged to a class. Saunders believes that this ordering of the questions encouraged people to say that they belonged to a particular class. Consequently, the results showed a high degree of class identification in the survey as a whole. This section of the questionnaire is reproduced in *Appendix B*, p.35. Turn to it now and examine questions 25 to 35. Do you agree with Saunders?

The criticisms made by Saunders illustrate two important aspects of how values influence sociological debate. Firstly, values affect how sociologists interpret data and evidence, for example, how we interpret absolute and relative rates of social mobility. Secondly, values affect the kinds of question that sociologists ask in the conduct of their research. Do you think that Marshall *et al.*'s socialist-egalitarian bias led them to load their questionnaire as Saunders suggests? Some of Saunders' detailed points are taken up by other critics discussed below.

Ray Pawson (1990) has argued that Marshall *et al.* are systematically biased in favour of the Goldthorpe model of class. Marshall *et al.* always look at the occupations of individuals, and judge whether they are typically working class or middle class. Occupations are the basis of the Goldthorpe scheme, so it is hardly surprising that they end up supporting Goldthorpe. Pawson points out that any abstract category, once it is applied, is bound to mis-allocate some individuals. Consequently, we should not expect any concept of class to be able to classify all individuals unambiguously.

Erik Olin Wright (1989) has made a similar point. He has argued that Marshall *et al.* have rejected his theory on the question of measurement when allocating people to classes, rather than on its explanatory power. He argues that Goldthorpe's theory and his theory share more similarities than differences in specifying who is middle class. In Wright's view Marshall *et al.* have focused too much on the details of how to measure social class rather than on the concepts of class used by different theorists (Wright, 1989, p.319).

Emmison and Western (1990) have argued that Marshall *et al.*'s questionnaire is biased, and make the following points, which are similar to those made by Saunders. Before people were asked about their class identity they had been asked many other questions about class, so they were 'primed' to give an answer about their identity in class terms (see questions numbered 25 to 32 in *Appendix B*). Furthermore, Marshall *et al.* did not give people sufficient opportunity to specify other possible sources of identity. Using similar data from Australia they found that class was not an important source of identity. Being a supporter of a sports club was found to be more important than class! In Emmison and Western's study *family, being an Australian, occupation* and *gender* were the most important sources of identity.

Fiona Devine has explored this criticism of Marshall *et al.*'s work using qualitative data from Luton car workers (Devine, 1992). (This was from a partial replication of Goldthorpe *et al.*'s *Affluent Worker* studies of the 1960s). She argues that people are readily able to draw upon their class identity in answering sociologists' questions. People often make reference to their class when explaining which way they vote, for example. But Devine shows that people have several social identities, and locality and nation or 'race' are just as important as class, among Luton car workers during the 1980s. Consequently, she rejects Marshall *et al.*'s strong claims about the overwhelming importance of class identity.

More recently Geoff Evans has re-analysed the data that Marshall *et al.* collected on class consciousness (Evans, 1992). He argues that their index of class consciousness, made up of six different attitude measurements, does not measure any coherent underlying class consciousness. Some of the attitude items in their index are about class, but others are not. Evans argues for a narrower measure of class consciousness, so that questions used in any index should be explicitly about class. In his re-analysis Evans found that education, trade union membership, age and income all affect class consciousness much more than Marshall *et al.* allowed.

The critical responses to Marshall *et al.*'s work have principally been methodological and concerned with their claims about the salience of class identities. In particular, critics have focused on the details of the procedures in their empirical analysis. Their broad theoretical conclusions have yet to be seriously challenged.

Bibliography

Devine, F. (1992), 'Social Identities, Class Identity and Political Perspectives' in *The Sociological Review*, Vol. 40, No. 2.

Emmison, M. and Western, M. (1990), 'Social Class and Social Identity: A Comment on Marshall *et al.*' in *Sociology*, Vol. 24, No. 2.

Evans, G. (1992), 'Is Britain a Class-Divided Society? A re-analysis and extension of Marshall *et al.*'s *Study of Class Consciousness*' in *Sociology*, Vol. 26, No. 2.

Goldthorpe, J. (1987), *Social Mobility and Class Structure in Modern Britain*, (second edition) Oxford, Clarendon Press.

Haralambos, M. (1991), *Sociology: themes and perspectives*, (third edition) (Chap. 2) London, Unwin Hyman.

Pawson, R. (1990), 'Half-Truths About Bias' in *Sociology*, Vol. 24, No. 2.

Saunders, P. (1989), 'Left Write' in *Network*, No. 44.

Saunders, P. (1990), *Social Class and Stratification*, London, Routledge.

Wright, E. O. (1989), 'Rethinking Once Again the Concept of Class Structure' in Wright, E. O. *et al.* (1989), *The Debate on Classes*, London, Verso.

Appendices

Appendix A

Table 3.1 Distribution of respondents into Registrar-General's class categories

Class		N	%
1	Professional, etc., occupations	48	3.7
2	Intermediate occupations	327	24.9
3N	Skilled occupations, nonmanual	294	22.4
3M	Skilled occupations, manual	358	27.2
4	Partly skilled occupations	212	16.1
5	Unskilled occupations	67	5.1
6	Armed forces	9	0.7
		1315	100.0

(Marshall *et al.*, 1988, Table 2.1)

Table 3.2 Distribution of respondents into Goldthorpe class categories

Class			N	%
Service	I	Higher-grade professionals, administrators, and officials; managers in large establishments; large proprietors.	123	9.4
	II	Lower-grade professionals, administrators, and officials; higher-grade technicians; managers in small business and industrial establishments; supervisors of nonmanual employees.	235	17.9
Intermediate	IIIa	Routine nonmanual employees in administration and commerce	198	15.1
	IIIb	Personal service workers	58	4.4
	IVa	Small proprietors, artisans, etc., with employees	45	3.4
	IVb	Small proprietors, artisans, etc., without employees	59	4.5
	IVc	Farmers and smallholders; self-employed fishermen	11	0.8
	V	Lower-grade technicians, supervisors of manual workers	107	8.1
Working	VI	Skilled manual workers	165	12.5
	VIIa	Semi-skilled and unskilled manual workers (not in agriculture)	307	23.4
	VIIb	Agricultural workers	7	0.5
			1315	100.0

(ibid., Table 2.2, p.22)

Table 3.3 Cross-classification of respondents into Registrar-General, Goldthorpe, and Wright class categories

A – Goldthorpe by Wright

		Bourgeoisie	Small employers	Petit bourgeoisie	Wright Managers and supervisors	Semi-autonomous employers	Workers	Total
Goldthorpe	I	1.4 (18)	0.5 (7)	0.3 (4)	6.1 (80)	0.5 (7)	0.5 (7)	9.4 (123)
	II	0.5 (6)	0.5 (6)	0.5 (7)	10.0 (132)	3.9 (51)	2.5 (33)	17.9 (235)
	III	0.0 (0)	0.0 (0)	0.0 (0)	2.4 (31)	4.1 (54)	13.0 (171)	19.5 (256)
	IV	0.2 (2)	3.4 (45)	5.2 (68)	0.0 (0)	0.0 (0)	0.0 (0)	8.7 (115)
	V	0.0 (0)	0.0 (0)	0.0 (0)	6.4 (84)	0.4 (5)	1.4 (18)	8.1 (107)
	VI	0.0 (0)	0.0 (0)	0.0 (0)	0.6 (8)	1.2 (16)	10.7 (141)	12.5 (165)
	VII	0.0 (0)	0.1 (1)	0.0 (0)	0.8 (11)	1.5 (20)	21.4 (282)	23.9 (314)
Total		2.0 (26)	4.5 (59)	6.0 (79)	26.3 (346)	11.6 (153)	49.6 (652)	100.0 (1315)

B - RG by Goldthorpe

		I	II	III	IV	V	VI	VII	Total
RG	1	3.7 (48)	0.0 (0)	0.0 (0)	0.0 (0)	0.0 (0)	0.0 (0)	0.0 (0)	3.7 (48)
	2	5.2 (68)	13.6 (179)	2.6 (34)	3.5 (46)	0.0 (0)	0.0 (0)	0.0 (0)	24.9 (327)
	3N	0.0 (0)	4.0 (53)	16.5 (217)	1.2 (16)	0.5 (7)	0.0 (0)	0.1 (1)	22.4 (294)
	3M	0.2 (3)	0.2 (3)	0.2 (3)	3.0 (39)	6.8 (89)	12.2 (161)	4.6 (60)	27.2 (358)
	4	0.0 (0)	0.0 (0)	0.2 (2)	0.8 (11)	0.5 (6)	0.3 (4)	14.4 (189)	16.1 (212)
	5	0.0 (0)	0.0 (0)	0.0 (0)	0.2 (3)	0.0 (0)	0.0 (0)	4.9 (64)	5.1 (67)
	6	0.3 (4)	0.0 (0)	0.0 (0)	0.0 (0)	0.4 (5)	0.0 (0)	0.0 (0)	0.7 (9)
Total		9.4 (123)	17.9 (235)	19.5 (256)	8.7 (115)	8.1 (107)	12.5 (165)	23.9 (314)	100.0 (1315)

C - RG by Wright

		Bourgeoisie	Small employers	Petit bourgeoisie	Wright Managers and supervisors	Semi-autonomous employers	Workers	Total
RG	1	0.4 (5)	0.4 (5)	0.2 (3)	2.1 (27)	0.3 (4)	0.3 (4)	3.7 (48)
	2	1.4 (18)	2.0 (26)	2.2 (29)	12.0 (158)	4.0 (53)	3.3 (43)	24.9 (327)
	3N	0.0 (0)	0.7 (9)	0.8 (10)	4.5 (59)	4.0 (52)	12.5 (164)	22.4 (294)
	3M	0.2 (3)	1.1 (14)	2.1 (27)	6.6 (87)	1.7 (22)	15.6 (205)	27.2 (358)
	4	0.0 (0)	0.3 (4)	0.6 (8)	0.5 (6)	1.6 (21)	13.2 (173)	16.1 (212)
	5	0.0 (0)	0.1 (1)	0.2 (2)	0.1 (1)	0.1 (1)	4.7 (62)	5.1 (67)
	6	0.0 (0)	0.0 (0)	0.0 (0)	0.6 (8)	0.0 (0)	0.1 (1)	0.7 (9)
Total		2.0 (26)	4.5 (59)	6.0 (79)	26.3 (346)	11.6 (153)	49.6 (652)	100.0 (1315)

Note: i Figures in brackets are raw numbers.

ii In this and some subsequent tables percentages may not add up exactly because of rounding.

(ibid., Table 2.5, p.28)

Table 3.4 Class on entry into employment by class of origin and sex (Goldthorpe class categories)

				Class on entry		
			Service	Intermediate	Working	Total
Class of origin	Service	Male	41	28	31	100 (105)
		Female	38	52	10	100 (98)
		All	39	39	21	100 (203)
	Intermediate	Male	18	25	57	100 (261)
		Female	18	60	22	100 (223)
		All	18	41	41	100 (484)
	Working	Male	12	16	72	100 (348)
		Female	10	53	37	100 (304)
		All	11	33	56	100 (562)
		All	18	37	45	100 (1339)

(ibid., Table 5.6, p.108)

Appendix B

A Section of the Questionnaire

15 Do you think the distribution of income and wealth in Britain is a fair one?

16 (a) Why don't you think it's fair?

(b) Can anything be done about this?

(c) What could be done?; or

(d) Why can nothing be done?

17 In recent years there have been considerable changes in government spending patterns. Have you or your immediate family been affected by changes in government spending on the National Health Service; education; law and order; public transport; council housing; unemployment benefit; supplementary benefit? Which of these has affected you or your immediate family most?

18 (a) Do you approve or disapprove of this?

(b) Have you done anything about it?

(c) What have you done?; or

(d) Why haven't you done anything?

19 Do you think it makes a great deal of difference which party runs the country?

20 Why do you feel it makes no difference?

21 If there were a general election tomorrow who would you vote for?

22 (a) Are there any particular reasons why you would vote for this party?

(b) What other kinds of people do you think vote for (this party) for the same reasons as yourself?

(c) Have you ever voted for another party at a general election?

(d) Which other party or parties have you voted for at past general elections?

Questionnaire *continued*

23 Outside of your normal work-time, do you take part in any of the types of groups on this [show card]?
24 Which ones?

Now some questions about social class.

25 (a) In the past there was a dominant class which largely controlled the economic and political system, and a lower class which had no control over economic or political affairs. Some people say that things are still like this, others say it has now changed. What do you think, has it changed, or stayed the same?
    (b) In what ways have things changed?
26 When you hear someone described as 'upper class' what sort of people do you think of?
27 When you hear someone described as 'middle class' what sort of person do you think of?
28 When you hear someone described as 'working class' what sort of person do you think of?
29 (a) How is it that people come to belong to the class that they do?
    (b) How do you feel about people belonging to a class because of birth, do you approve or disapprove?
    (c) Do you think it is easy or hard for a person to go from one social class to another?
    (d) Under what circumstances do you think a person could move from one class to another?
30 (a) Do you think there are any important issues which cause conflicts between social classes?
    (b) What conflicts are these?
31 Do you think class is an inevitable feature of modern society?
32 Do you think of yourself as belonging to any particular social class?
33 Suppose you were asked to say which class you belonged to, which would you say?
34 Apart from class, is there any other major group you identify with?
35 (a) What sort of group are you thinking of?
    (b) Do you normally think of yourself as a member of that grouping or as a member of a social class?

(ibid., pp.294–295)

4

The Political Sociology of Voting Behaviour

Anthony Heath *et al.*, *Understanding Political Change: The British Voter 1964–87*, 1991, Oxford, Pergamon.

Colin Hay

The Sociology of Voting

In recent years the sociology of the voting behaviour of the British electorate has emerged as a hotly debated and, indeed, highly contentious area of study. With the existence of meticulous empirical evidence in the form of the British Election Survey dating back to the 1964 election, it has been possible to study in immense detail the changing political loyalties of the electorate. In seeking to understand and explain changes in political attitudes, sociologists have uncovered relatively strong and more-or-less consistent correlations between the social characteristics of the voter (notably social class, ethnic group, religion, education, age, housing tenure and trade union membership) and electoral preference. In so doing they have built up a complex picture of the political sociology of the British electorate since the 1960s.

Social variables, however, cannot account *entirely* for the success or failure of a political party's appeal to the electorate and performance at the polls. Perhaps, as a consequence, much of the debate has revolved around the question of the relative importance of social and political variables in determining electoral outcomes.

Particularly important in this regard has been the debate surrounding the question of *class dealignment*. Advocates of the class dealignment thesis (see for instance Crewe, 1984; Dunleavy and Husbands, 1985) have argued that there has been a withering away of social class as a key predictor of voting behaviour. This is a consequence, they suggest, of widescale social change in post-war Britain with:

- increasing upward social mobility;
- the spread of home-ownership; and
- the decline of densely unionized heavy industries.

The result of this, it has been argued, is that the Labour Party's traditional constituency amongst the 'old' working class has simply evaporated, and that this explains the poor electoral performance of the Labour Party, particularly since 1979. For, not only has the Labour Party now suffered four consecutive election defeats (in 1979, 1983, 1987 and 1992), but in each of these elections it has failed to poll over 40% of the vote with its vote slumping to 28% in 1983 and 31% in 1987. Dissenters from this view (see Heath *et al.*, 1985; Goldthorpe, 1987; Marshall *et al.*, 1988) have argued that there has in fact been no such dealignment and that although the *size* of the working class has declined, its loyalties and attitudes have remained relatively unaltered. Labour's electoral misfortune should thus be interpreted in terms of the combination of two factors: (i) the decline in size of Labour's core constituency in the traditional working class; and (ii) Labour's political difficulties. Put simply, they argue, Labour is still a class party, but a less successful one.

Understanding Political Change is the most comprehensive and up-to-date contribution to this debate, by a group of very experienced and respected *psephologists* (those who study voting behaviour), now responsible for the British Election Study (BES). It considers the changing voting patterns of the British electorate since 1964 with the benefit of the new information offered by the 1987 BES. In particular it focuses upon three crucial issues:

- The volatility of the electorate; has the electorate in fact become more or less volatile since the 1960s?
- The possible emergence of new social cleavages, perhaps replacing those of social class
- The impact of the radical policies of the Thatcher Governments upon the social structure of contemporary Britain and upon voting patterns

Research Design

In their research Heath *et al.* draw upon the British Election Surveys that were started in 1963 and have taken place immediately after each subsequent general election. There has been a substantial degree of continuity and a common core of questions asked in each of the surveys, and, as a consequence, the British Election Surveys represent 'the longest academic series of nationally representative probability sample surveys in this country' (Heath *et al.*, 1991, p.225). The data were collected in each of the surveys through extensive interviews with a representative cross-section of the British electorate (excluding Northern Ireland).

The surveys have also included a panel element consisting of repeat interviews with respondents who have been interviewed in a previous survey. This allows for some direct analysis of changes in individual attitudes between elections and is an important supplement to the cross-sectional survey. This sort of data is particularly useful in assessing, for instance, the changing attitudes of former council tenants after purchasing their own homes under the Thatcher government's 'Right to Buy' scheme.

The consistent aim of the British Election Surveys has been to provide a data set from which to explore the changing determinants of electoral behaviour in contemporary Britain. The surveys have each included questions on electoral behaviour; political participation and party identification; broader social and political attitudes; and both objective and subjective biographical data regarding education, housing, social class, trade union membership, ethnic group, religion, marital status, age, etc. The large sample size (varying between 2000 and 4000 respondents) and the range of the variables makes this an immensely valuable data set which is rich in resources for both cross-sectional and time-series analyses correlating social and political variables.

Principal Findings

In summarizing the multitude of important results that this extensive historical study has thrown up, it is useful to organize the results into three categories reflecting the initial questions posed by the researchers: (i) electoral volatility; (ii) the case for the 'withering away of class' and the emergence of new social and political cleavages; and (iii) the impact of Thatcherism upon the social structure and voting patterns of the British electorate.

(i) *Electoral volatility*

The major finding of *Understanding Political Change* on the issue of electoral volatility leads Heath *et al.* to challenge the claim put forward by Ivor Crewe and others of the 'secularization of party choice' or 'partisan dealignment' (see Crewe, Sarlvik and Alt, 1977; Crewe, 1984). This view suggests that the British electorate has become more open and volatile and more inclined to vote on the basis of specific issues, the personalities of the leaders, the appeal of the parties during election campaigns, and the record of the government in office, as opposed to any enduring or 'natural' alignments to specific parties.

Heath *et al.* argue that such a view simply cannot be sustained through a detailed anlysis of their data. Using a variety of indices of overall volatility they suggest that there has been no clear trend towards increased electoral volatility. Rather, they claim, 'trendless fluctuation might seem to be a sensible way to characterize the pattern or rather the lack of pattern' (ibid., p.20).

Whilst Heath *et al.* do observe a gradual decline in party identification since the 1960s they go on to argue that if it is seen as a measure of the satisfaction of the voter with their party, then a decline in identification need not necessarily lead to increased volatility if opposing parties have similarly become less attractive. Furthermore, even these relatively minor trends in volatility may be accounted for as the product of political changes, instead of some broader transformation of the social psychology of the electorate as suggested by the thesis of partisan dealignment. For, they argue, volatility is likely to be greater in a stable three-party system (where transfers between the centre party and the parties of the left and right are likely to be common) than in a stable two-party system. One of the key political changes since the 1960s has been precisely such a shift from a two- to a three-party system, and hence we should not be looking for explanations in terms of the changing pyschology of the voter when a far more obvious political explanation presents itself.

Similarly, when it comes to the question of tactical voting, the small increase in the total amount of tactical voting should not be explained in terms of a more rational, sophisticated and calculating electorate (as suggested by the theorists of partisan dealignment), but in terms of the increased possibilities for tactical voting opened up by the greater number and success of Liberal/Alliance candidates.

The picture that emerges, therefore, is of an electorate that has not really changed in terms of its social psychology – its sophistication, rationality or partisan alignment – but one which is forced to make political decisions in the changed political context of a three-party system that favours volatility and tactical voting.

(ii) *The 'withering away of class' and the emergence of new social and political cleavages?*

The question of the withering away of class as a key determinant of the voting patterns of the electorate has a long and acrimonious history. In *Understanding Political Change*, Heath *et al.* re-nail their flag to the proverbial mast, confirming and restating their earlier conclusions and those of Marshall *et al.* (Heath *et al.*, 1985; Marshall *et al.*, 1988):

> Our findings do not support the popular belief that we are witnessing a long-term decline in class loyalties and attitudes. Just as the structural processes associated with class have persisted into the late twentieth century, in the face of sustained attempts at egalitarian reform by successive governments in post-war Britain, so too have the ideological differences associated with a class-based culture. (Marshall *et al.*, 1988, p.182, cited in Heath *el al.*, 1991, p.63)

Heath *et al.* find that whilst the level of *absolute* class voting (defined as the overall proportion of voters supporting their 'natural' class party[1]) has indeed fallen, the level of *relative* class voting (referring to the *relative* strength of the parties in different social classes – the class composition of the parties' vote) has remained relatively constant.[2] Thus they observe no weakening of the *strength of the relationship* between class and vote although they do highlight the falling size of the working class and the predicament that this generates for the Labour Party. They discover that subjective perceptions of class identification have not dramatically changed since the 1960s (see *Table 4.1*, p.47) and that the Labour Party still retains a considerable working class support, though in recent years it has lost votes from all classes alike. This is explained by Heath *et al.* in terms of a combination of political factors and the decline in size of the working class, as opposed to class dealignment. Hence, Labour's misfortune at the polls is seen as a product of the increasing number of seats contested by the Liberals/Alliance, the failure of the Labour governments of the 1970s to satisfy their supporters and the decline in the size of Labour's traditional working class constituency.

In terms of the emergence of new social cleavages, Heath *et al.* consider the evidence for the growth of new cleavages within both the salariat (the professional middle class) and the working class. In so doing they discover the emergence of a 'new middle class' comprised of professional employees in the public sector which is increasingly differentiated in terms of ideology and interest from the old middle class of managers and businessmen. What emerges therefore is a picture of a divided salariat, differentiated in relation to political preference according to education, public or private sector employment and trade union membership. The 'new middle class' is predominantly composed of relatively highly educated and unionized public sector employees and is electorally quite homogeneous, being more inclined to vote for Liberal/Alliance and Labour candidates than their peers in the traditional middle class. This new middle class Labour vote is characterized by the anti-materialist values of what Heath *et al.* term the 'New Left' which prioritize quality of life over economic growth. This suggests a possible difficulty for Labour in trying to reconcile the conflicting interests of this salariat 'New Left' and its traditional 'Old Left' core constituency amongst the unionized working class.

Amongst the working class, the cleavages that Heath *et al.* observe are less pronounced. This is despite a plethora of recent research that has suggested the importance of new cleavages within the working class based upon public or private sector employment, reliance upon state welfare benefits, and housing tenure (Dunleavy and Husbands, 1985; Crewe, 1987; Edgell and Duke, 1991). Heath *et al.* find that the political differences between public and private sector employees are in fact rather modest, leading them to reject the argument for a new 'sectoral' cleavage within the working class. Similarly, whilst they do observe a significant relationship between housing tenure and voting patterns within the working class, with owner occupiers being more inclined to vote Conservative, this relationship is no stronger than it was in 1964. Labour's vote has plummeted amongst owner occupiers and local authority tenants alike. As a consequence they conclude, 'it is clear that the spread of owner-occupation within the working class cannot explain to any great extent why the Labour vote within the working class has crumbled' (ibid., p.107). The same is also true of regional and ethnic differences which continue to fragment the working-class to roughly the same extent that they did in the 1960s. To summarize, Heath *et al.* do find that Labour and Conservative voters amongst the working class are closer together, both in terms of their social profiles and their attitudes, than are the salariat. Nevertheless they do observe a working class fragmented by region, ethnicity, and housing tenure. However they find little evidence of *growing* sectoral cleavages within the working class which might explain Labour's decline.

(iii) *The impact of Thatcherism*

The third basic set of issues addressed in *Understanding Political Change* concerns the impact of the policies pursued by the Thatcher governments on the social structure of contemporary Britain and the consequences that this has had upon the voting behaviour of the electorate. As we have seen Heath *et al.* reject the more sociological and psychological explanations for changing voting patterns in terms of class and partisan dealignment and the emergence of new social cleavages. Hence they are drawn to consider the impact of political changes and in so doing concentrate upon:

- the extension of 'popular capitalism' through the selling-off of council housing and the doubling of share ownership in Britain since 1979; and
- the influence of what Stuart Hall has termed Thatcher's 'authoritarian populist' appeal to the electorate (Hall, 1979).

Heath *et al.* observe that both home and share ownership display a close correlation with Conservative voting (see *Tables 4.3* and *4.4*, p.48). However, they go on to suggest that it does not necessarily follow from this that individuals will become more inclined to vote Conservative when they purchase their own homes or buy shares in newly privatized industries. Their alternative explanation is that those inclined to become owner occupiers and share-owners are *already* more likely to be Conservative voters in the first place, concluding that

> our analysis fails ... to show that privatization *per se* had any electoral impact on the purchasers. In particular, the new recruits have neither rewarded the Tories for their windfall gains nor become more attached to the economic order. Claims about the effects of popular capitalism simply failed to recognize that the share purchasers were not a random selection of the electorate in the first place. (ibid., pp.125–6)

A similar conclusion is reached in relation to council housing sales. Heath *et al.* find that purchasers do vote differently from non-purchasers. However, they were already more prone to vote Conservative in 1979 and hence there is little evidence to suggest that the sale of council housing has produced new recruits for the Tories. Yet despite this evidence, they do find that the Labour vote has dropped more swiftly among purchasers than other groups. Thus they cannot entirely reject the hypothesis that council-house purchases might have had some minor impact upon political attitudes. Stuart Hall has suggested that Mrs Thatcher's initial appeal to the electorate was not purely based upon the right-wing economics of privatization and the free-market, but also upon what he terms 'authoritarian populism' (Hall, 1979). This refers to Thatcher's crusading moral rhetoric associated with tradition, authority and the reasssertion of moral and ethical 'standards'. Heath *et al.* consider to what extent Thatcher's crusade to change social and moral values has proved effective. In so doing they construct two axes of opinion and attitude:

(1) a *left-right dimension* which refers to attitudes towards income redistribution, nationalization and privatization, the regulation of trade unions, expenditure on the NHS, etc.; and
(2) a *liberal-authoritarian dimension* which refers to attitudes towards ethnic minorities, the death penalty, the sentencing of convicted criminals, the availability of abortion on the NHS, etc.

The results of their analysis are summarised in *Tables 4.3* and *4.4*, p.48. These very interesting data are somewhat difficult to interpret. Initially it appears that, in relation to the left-right dimension, the electorate has actually moved to the left on certain issues and that Mrs Thatcher's crusade has been something of a disaster. However, when the extent of the changes in trade union legislation and welfare reform enacted under the Thatcher governments is considered, it is more likely, as Heath *et al.* point out, that the electorate has simply stayed in the same place and the world has changed around it. Clearly, for instance, the leftward drift of responses to the question of whether the government should introduce stricter laws to regulate trade union activity might merely reflect the fact that throughout the 1980s stricter regulations have been brought into existence. To say that we need stricter laws today is clearly very different to saying that we needed stricter laws in 1974. Thus, we should be very careful about interpreting these results as evidence of a rejection of Thatcher's radical programme of reforms. Furthermore, on the issues of public ownership and income redistribution, the government appears to have been somewhat more successful: both declined in popularity at a time when the public sector has been radically reduced and patterns of social inequality greatly amplified. Here the Thatcher governments do appear to have had some impact in transforming the attitudes of the electorate, stimulating an acceptance of the principles of the free market, 'popular capitalism' and a reduced role for the public sector.

In relation to the liberal-authoritarian dimension there appears to have been little overall change in attitudes and certainly no clear evidence emerges of the electorate becoming increasingly authoritarian in response to Thatcher's authoritarian populist appeal. Heath *et al.* conclude that Thatcher's 'authoritarian populism' has failed to gain her votes and that the real story is one of 'the Conservatives

strengthening their position in their existing strongholds, whether
defined in economic or ideological terms, rather than making converts
in foreign territory' (ibid., 180).

Critical Observations

Though not yet subject to extended critical scrutiny, reviews of
Understanding Political Change have been generally extremely
favourable (Harrop, 1991; Warde, 1992).

Nevertheless there have been a number of pertinent criticisms levied
at the argument presented by Heath *et al.*

Firstly there is not a little irony in the fact that sociologists such as
Heath should produce such a detailed attempted debunking of many
of the psephological explanations for contemporary political change in
Britain. For such accounts often provide somewhat more sociological
explanations, expressed in terms of class or partisan dealignment and
the emergence of new sectoral cleavages within the working class. It
thus seems ironic that a sociologist should apparently be looking for
political explanations, whilst the political scientists are busy search-
ing for sociological explanations! This is hinted at most strongly by
Harrop when he chastises Heath *et al.* for what he sees as their failure
to get to the heart of the regional differences in the voting patterns
of the working class, which must, by their very nature require some
sort of sociological explanation. As he suggests, Heath *et al.* fail to
explain the changing geographical dimension of voting, enjoying little
success in trying to account for such well-documented processes as the
collapse of the working class Labour vote in the south, by reference to
the changing social composition of the regions. Harrop concludes

> The North-South divide is a hard nut to crack in electoral studies but it
> surely needs to be explained, rather than explained away. (Harrop, 1991,
> p.601)

This leads us on to a second commonly expressed criticism of *Understanding Political Change* – that, despite providing an immensely detailed descriptive account of contemporary social and political change
and the political sociology of today's electors, their work is rather short
on explanation. What we are offered is a rejection of the orthodox analyses which have sought to explain contemporary electoral change in
terms of class dealignment, electoral volatility and an increasingly
rational and sophisticated electorate, but we are offered very little in
its place. For instance, as Harrop again suggests, whilst *Understanding Political Change* 'is not a nit-picking book . . . it [does] debunk text
book clichés rather more effectively than it develops its own interpretation of electoral behaviour' (Harrop, 1991, p.601). This is perhaps a
little unfair, for whilst Heath *et al.* certainly do not come up with a
single overall mechanism of change whilst debunking several such
hypotheses, they do provide a rather convincing *explanation* for

continuity. Their analysis is, in this sense, neither short of interpretation nor explanation.

Warde (1992), on the other hand, is rather more convinced by their arguments for continuity, suggesting that they successfully expose the limitations of the existing orthodox views of social and political change. What this demonstrates, he argues, is that we do not really require a general theory of the changing social psychology or social composition of the electorate in order to explain the nature of political change since the 1960s. For many of the processes supposedly explained by such theories have been grossly exaggerated in the first place. Consequently 'it is parties changing their strategies that accounts for political flux rather than change in the electorate' (Warde, 1992, pp.147–8).

What must surely be agreed upon, however, is that, as Harrop again suggests, *Understanding Political Change*, despite drawing upon the most comprehensive data collected on the 1987 general election, can offer us very little in the way of an explanation as to why the Tories managed to win. What we are offered is a vague sense that the orthodox analyses of psephologists cannot be stretched to explain the Tories' third electoral victory in a row, and that we must look towards the strategies pursued by the individual parties. Yet precisely how long-term social and political changes and the specific strategies pursued by the parties conspired to produce the actual result remains something of a mystery.

Finally, it is important to note that despite providing the most comprehensive and extensive coverage of processes of political change in Britain since the 1960s, there is a glaring omission from their analysis – the question of gender. Surprisingly Heath *et al.* offer us no analysis of the changing impact of gender upon voting behaviour. What makes this even more disappointing is the recent interest in this question stimulated by scholars such as Goot and Reid, Dunleavy and Husbands, and Campbell who have looked in great detail at the disproportionately large Conservative vote amongst women, and evidence of its recent decline (Goot and Reid, 1984; Dunleavy and Husbands, 1985; Campbell, 1987). It is clearly something of a missed opportunity that such findings, which might have been expected to shed considerable light upon processes of political change since the 1960s, have not been investigated and incorporated into this otherwise comprehensive study.

Conclusion

Understanding Political Change provides an extremely detailed, sophisticated and meticulous insight into the processes of political change in Britain since the 1960s. It makes a highly convincing case for continuity as opposed to wholesale change. In so doing, it challenges the more orthodox theories which point to a transformation of the social psychology of the voter, resulting in increased electoral volatility and a rational and sophisticated electorate, voting increasingly on the basis of issues and personalities, as opposed to more deeply entrenched political attitudes and ideologies. It similarly questions more sociological analyses which point to class dealignment and the emergence of new sectoral cleavages within the working class resulting in a fragmentation of Labour's traditional core constituency.

Instead it suggests that in seeking to understand contemporary political change we should look to a combination of:

(i) the changing social composition of the electorate – the decline in size of the working class, the rise in owner-occupation, and the increasing secularization of British society; and
(ii) short-term reversible political factors such as the growth in number of Liberal/Alliance candidates, the strategies pursued by the parties, and the performance of the government.

Notes

[1] For the working-class taken to be Labour, for the middle-class taken to be the Conservatives.

[2] Consider a situation in which the Labour Party were to lose support from all classes, equally. It would thus still retain its previous class profile but would simply have gained less votes from all classes alike. This is an example of a decrease in *absolute* class voting (since the number of electors voting for their 'natural' class party has declined) yet there would have been no decrease in *relative* class voting since the class composition of Labour's vote would have remained unaltered.

Bibliography and Further Reading

Abercrombie, N. and Warde, A. *et al.* (1988), *Contemporary British Society*, Cambridge, Polity.

Campbell, B. (1987), *The Iron Ladies*, London, Virago.

Crewe, I., Sarlvik, B. and Alt, J. (1977), 'Partisan Dealignment in Britain, 1964–74,' in *British Journal of Political Science*, Vol.7, pp.129–190.

Crewe, I. (1984), 'The Electorate: Partisan Dealignment Ten Years On', in Berrington, H. (ed.), *Change in British Politics*, London, Frank Cass.

Crewe, I. (1987), 'A New Class of Politics?' *The Guardian*, 15 June.

Dunleavy, P. and Husbands, C.T. (1985), *British Democracy at the Crossroads*, London, Allen & Unwin.

Edgell, S. and Duke, V. (1991), *A Measure of Thatcherism*, London, Harper Collins.

Goldthorpe, J.H. (1987), *Social Mobility and Class Structure in Modern Britain*, Oxford, Clarendon Press.

Goot, M. and Reid, E. (1984), 'Women: If Not Apolitical then Conservative', in Stanworth, M. and Siltanen, J. (eds.), *Women and the Public Sphere*, London, Hutchinson.

Hal, S. (1979), 'The Great Moving Right Show,' reprinted in Hall, S. and Jacques, M. (eds.), *Thatcherism*, London, Lawrence & Wishart.

Harrop, M. (1991), 'Elections and Voters,' *Parliamentary Affairs*, Vol. 4, pp.600–5.

Heath, A. *et al.* (1985), *How Britain Votes*, Oxford, Pergamon.

Marshall, G. *et al.* (1988), *Social Class in Modern Britain*, London, Hutchinson.

Warde, A. (1992), Review of 'Understanding Political Change' in *Sociology*, Vol. 26, No. 1, pp.147–8.

Appendices

Table 4.1 Subjective Perceptions of Class 1964–87

	% who described themseves as . . .				
	Middle class	Working class	don't know		N
1964	29	66	5	100%	887
1966	30	66	4	100%	1860
1970	33	63	4	100%	732
Feb 1974	33	63	4	100%	2443
Oct 1974	33	62	4	99%	2341
1979	33	62	5	100%	1849
1983	34	59	6	99%	3897
1987	34	62	4	100%	3795

(Heath *et al*, Table 5.8, p.75)

Table 4.2 Le Patrimoine (an individual's stake in the country's wealth)

	Vote in 1987				
	Cons	Lab	Other	Did not	N
Home- and share-owner	55	12	22	11	1005
Home-owners w/o shares	38	25	22	16	1589
Share-owners in rented property	33	30	20	17	132
Non-owners	20	45	45	16	963

(ibid., Table 8.2, p.122)

Tables 4.3 and *4.4* Changing Left-Right and Liberal-Authoritarian Attitudes

% agreeing that the government should:	Left-Right Attitudes			
	Oct 1974	1979	1983	1987
Redistribute income and wealth to ordinary working people	54	52	48	50
Spend more money to get rid of poverty	84	80	81	86
Nationalize more companies	30	16	16	16
Privatize some companies	20	38	38	31
Not introduce stricter laws to regulate TUs	—	16	32	33
Give workers more say in running places where they work	58	55	68	76
Put more money into the NHS	84	87	85	90
% agreeing that:				
Welfare benefits have gone too far	22	17	28	34

% agreeing that:	Liberal-Authoritarian Attitudes			
	1974	1979	1983	1987
Right to show nudity and sex in films gone too far	63	65	62	65
Availability of abortion on the NHS has gone too far	40	41	27	28
The attempt to give equal opportunities to blacks has gone too far	26	28	18	28
The Government should not give more aid to poor countries	46	47	—	42
Britain should bring back the death penalty	—	69	56	74
People who break the law should be given stiffer sentances	95	90	77	80

(ibid., Tables 11.3 and 11.4, pp.176–7)

5

Consumption, Social Inequality and the Extension of Home Ownership

Peter Saunders (1990), *A Nation of Home Owners*, London, Unwin Hyman.

Alan Warde

Housing Tenure and Social Inequality

Since the late 19th century, the majority view among sociologists was that class was the primary social division in capitalist societies. The ownership of property and access to occupations with different levels of reward were the principal sources of inequality. During the 1980s, it became common to argue that the importance of class was diminishing. Some suggested that the experience of work and economic production was becoming less central to people's lives and that, instead, consumption – how they spent their money and their free time – had become their main preoccupation. It was suggested that this was creating new, distinctive, systematic inequalities, between people in different *consumption sectors* (e.g. Dunleavy, 1980; Saunders, 1986; Edgell and Duke, 1991). In particular, such a division, or 'consumption sector cleavage', was said to have developed between, on the one hand, people dependent on publicly provided services and, on the other hand, those more affluent persons who buy privately their own houses, medical care, transport, education, etc. One outcome was said to be social polarisation as the material conditions of these two categories of people diverged, the first group becoming increasingly impoverished. Also anticipated was a change in political alignments; as a significant proportion of working class people gained access to private means of consumption, solidarities based in shared material disadvantage might be eroded.

This argument was most widely developed and debated with regard to housing provision. The expansion of owner-occupied housing is one of the most dramatic trends of the 20th century. In 1910 about one household in ten owned the house that they lived in and the other 90%

lived in privately rented accommodation. In subsequent decades more people bought their own houses and the state, as part of its local welfare policies, built houses which were publicly-owned and available for rent. Consequently, the private-rented sector diminished enormously. By 1991, 66% of British households either owned outright, or were buying on a mortgage, their home. A further 21% lived in council houses and 7% in privately rented property.

The percentage of owner-occupiers increased significantly during the 1980s as a result of central government instructions to local authorities that they should sell, at large discounts, council houses to sitting tenants and prohibiting the building of replacements. As a consequence, over one million council houses were sold and thus became owner-occupied This policy was politically controversial for, though popular with tenants, it symbolised for many a determination to cut back state welfare provision, a major plank of the 'Thatcherite' programme of 'privatization'.

The political debate inspired renewed interest among social scientists in the social and political implications of housing tenure. Peter Saunders was especially concerned with the comparative benefits of market versus state provision of housing. He was unusual in his largely unqualified defence of markets as mechanisms to regulate production, distribution and exchange in the field of housing. *A Nation of Home Owners* reported a survey-based study of issues relevant to the debate including: the motivations involved in house purchase; its benefits, both material and psychological; whether owner-occupation affected people's political attitudes and voting behaviour; and whether owners were particularly detached from collective involvement and likely to lead private daily lives. The findings were used to examine contrasting sociological arguments about the impact of owner-occupation.

Research Design

Saunders conducted interviews in 450 households, 150 in each of three towns, Slough, Derby and Burnley, places chosen because they had different histories of economic development, housing policy and house price inflation. In 72 of those households two people were interviewed, resulting in a total sample of 522 individuals. The interviewees were principal householders, either men or women, who lived in a family house (i.e. shared households, flats and cardboard boxes were excluded). All were either council tenants or owner-occupiers – tenants in privately-rented accommodation and housing association members were also omitted from consideration. In each town interviews took place with 50 households in each of three different types of housing area. Type A was a suburban neighbourhood with a high proportion of semi-detached houses in the upper half of the price range. Type B comprised mainly terraced houses near the centre of the town and at the lower end of price range (much of which was pre-1919 housing stock). Type C comprised council accommodation, the sample being taken from both the best and the worst estates in each town, irrespective of whether people had recently bought their houses. As a matter of fact, many houses on the first kind of estate (post-1945 and containing few flats) had been bought, few of the latter type (pre-war usually). The questionnaire was of the structured type but included a lot of open-ended questions. The response rate was 'disappointing' (Saunders, 1990, p.379), with only about 50% of those approached agreeing to be interviewed.

Principal Findings

(i) *The desire to own*

One contentious issue concerns the reasons for the sharply increased demand for owner-occupation in the second half of the 20th century. Saunders argues that it is partly a historical accident, partly a deep-rooted preference for personal ownership. Consistent with other recent surveys, virtually all Saunders' respondents expressely preferred to be owner-occupiers. The reasons people gave for deciding to become owner-occupiers are summarised in *Table 5.1*, p.58. Saunders concludes from this that there are two principal motivations: one is financial, the other 'has to do with the sense of independence and autonomy that ownership confers' (ibid., p.84). He judged that the first of these motives 'probably outweighs the second'.

(a) material gains and the structure of inequality

Saunders provides evidence that people believe that owner-occupation confers a financial gain and he demonstrates that this belief is true. He argues that almost all owner-occupiers, whether in cheap or expensive houses, make real gains on their property, that they are powerfully conscious of the possibilities of making money from home ownership, and that people can and do cash in their gains. Wealth accumulation occurs, with gains proportionate to the price of the house and the length of time spent in owner-occupation. Thus Saunders observes that 'two employees on the same income could therefore end up with very different economic situations according to whether or not they own their own homes.' (ibid., p.122)

The implication is that working class people in particular are no longer solely dependant on wages, that they have come to be owners of property themselves, and that thereby the importance of social class position as a determinant of material affluence is reduced. This might be expected to have long-term consequences as property, or its money equivalent, is transmitted from parents to their children. Sons and daughters of working class owner- occupiers might anticipate substantial inheritances. As Saunders puts it, 'if nearly two thirds of the population are now in a position to accumulate and pass on large sums of money through ownership of domestic property, then our theories of social inequality and class stratification may need revising.' (ibid., p.203)

(b) the sense of ownership

Saunders is equally concerned to demonstrate that ownership gives people a sense of autonomy and security. He quotes some of his respondents to this effect:

> 'You can do what you like with it. It's worth decorating – I'm going to knock that wall out. It's a feeling of freedom to do what you like in it and have who you want in it.'
>> (Male, intermediate occupation, Slough, ibid., pp.86–7)

> 'It's a sense of security. And if you've got children you've got something to leave them.'
>> (Female, skilled manual worker, Derby, ibid., p.88)

Overall, 39% of respondents mentioned the ability to 'do what they liked' with their own houses as an advantage of owner occupation, 13% mentioned security of tenure and another 12% pride of ownership. These attractions of owner-occupation may be the consequence of strong dissatisfaction with tenancy, arising from the paternalism of landlords and the inability of the tenant to alter or dispose of the house occupied. *Table 5.2*, p.58 indicates people's perceptions of the advantages and disadvantages of council house renting. Saunders therefore concludes that the benefits of ownership, material gain and independence, are inherent to the tenure form. Rented property can *never* give people the things that they consider council housing to lack. Hence the decision of people to buy their council houses is entirely rational, as indeed is the desire to be an owner more generally.

(ii) Political consequences of owner-occupation

The Thatcher government believed that its policy of council house sales would have electoral benefits because home-owners more frequently vote Conservative than do council tenants. This statistical relationship has been interpreted as evidence of the increasing importance of a voter's consumption sector over his or her class position. Indeed, Saunders (1986) had earlier argued strongly that sectoral cleavages were emerging as the relationship diminished between class and party choice (class dealignment). In *A Nation of Home Owners*, however, he came to a different conclusion, showing that sociologists do change their minds as a result of carrying out empirical research!

Evidence from the three towns shows that while private ownership is related to voting behaviour, if we take into account the social class to which people belong, consumption sector matters little. In other words, class position tends to determine the consumption sector in which a person is located. Sectoral divisions thus explain neither the origins of class dealignment nor the subsequent patterns of voting. Nevertheless, Saunders maintains that there are real material interests which divide home-owners from tenants. Owner-occupiers, for instance, tend to join residents' associations to protect their financial investments. The tacit agreement of all political parties not to interfere with mortgage tax-relief, the very basis of the economic advantages of home ownership, is also evidence of the powerful, established interests of owner-occupiers.

(iii) *Privatism*

Another issue in the debate about home-ownership has concerned whether new social attitudes develop along with the private ownership of houses. Saunders examines some contested claims about the meaning of home-ownership. He begins from the premise that 'the home is the core institution in our society' and the household its distinctive form of organization (ibid., p.266). He shows that, symbolically, the idea of the home is associated with family life, emotional and physical security, and ownership of the dwelling. Generally, people expressed very positive sentiments about their homes. There is not much difference between men and women in terms of their responses to the meaning of home, their satisfaction with their houses, or even their opportunities for going out.

However, he is sceptical, partly on the basis of historical evidence, partly because of his survey findings, of the argument that owner occupation induces 'privatism'. He makes a useful distinction between '*private property* (a socio-legal term denoting rights of exclusive use, control and disposal), *privatism* (defined as withdrawal or detachment from active participation in collective life) and *privacy* or the "private realm" (denoting freedom from surveillance by others)' (ibid., p.274). Saunders explores the growth of privatism.

He provides some evidence that home-ownership reduces neighbourhood relations (see *Table 5.3*). Mutual aid and neighbourliness is, overall, stronger on council estates. However, this may be due to different rates of geographical mobility. Tenants were less mobile, 80% having never lived in any other town than their present one, compared with 50% of owner-occupiers. Also, tenants had lived in their existing houses longer on average. He finds that people in the North are more inclined to consider the neighbourhood in which they live as important, and that the further north the more friendly the neighbourhood is considered.

However, owner-occupiers are *more* involved in local organizations, even when we control for social class. That is to say, both middle class and working class owner-occupiers are more likely than others in their own class to join voluntary associations. This finding may, however, be the result of working class tenants being older, on average, than owner-occupiers and thus less active.

There is no statistical relationship between tenure and whether people go out for their entertainment. No evidence emerged that mortgagees are so heavily burdened by debt that they cannot afford to go out; and only the occasional instance was discovered of people who consciously change their behaviour to become home-centred as a result of acquiring their own home. Saunders therefore finds the link between owner-occupation and privatism tenuous at best.

(iv) *Polarization: the fate of tenants*

Saunders also speculates about the future plight of the non-home owner seeing tenure as the basis of 'stark polarization' (ibid., p.315). Since tenants who are currently purchasing their houses are the richer ones, in future we might anticipate even greater material inequalities between people in the public rented sector and owner-occupiers. Saunders argues that this must have effects on the class structure. He maintains that class position is not the only factor 'shaping access to home-ownership' and that 'patterns of consumption of housing may themselves contribute to inequalities of life chances', largely because of the capital gains argument. Exploring ways of incorporating this into our understanding of stratification, he argues that we must recognise 'whether and how people's material circumstances and personal lives are shaped by the intervention of the state'. This fits housing well, for 'the two tenures have come to be distinguished by a differentiation of life chances which is grounded as much in the use of state power as in existing class inequalities' (ibid., p.334). He asserts that 'the defining feature of the underclass is not so much its exclusion from owner-occupation (although this is important) as its dependency on state provision across *all* aspects of life including its housing' (ibid., p.335).

Evaluation

(1) This is an important book, bearing on many current sociological arguments. It offers a powerful challenge to a range of orthodox sociological presuppositions about housing, welfare, privatization and stratification. It is, thus, inherently controversial. It is made more so because Saunders has been outspoken in criticism of what he sees as a left-wing bias in British sociology. Certainly that claim is not without foundation in the field of housing studies, if support for public housing is taken as the yardstick of a left consensus.

Most critics observe that his 'overzealous' or 'evangelical' attitude to mass home-ownership detracts from the serious and sober argumentation of the substantive sections of the book (e.g. Hamnett, 1991; Forrest, 1991; Harloe, 1992). Certainly, the introductory and concluding sections to most chapters tend to be polemics against Marxist positions. Thus, judgments about the book are clouded by the political and ideological overtones of the position that Saunders espouses; those with New Right sympathies tend to welcome the book as a great step forward for sociology, while those of leftist persuasion pronounce it unorthodox and unsubstantiated.

(2) Perhaps because it so overtly challenged the consensus about housing policy, the methodology of the survey has been subject to particular scrutiny. Reservations are numerous. The low rate of response has caused concern (Harloe, 1992), particularly as the sample seemed to under-represent skilled working class respondents, a key group in the arguments about class, housing and voting (Byrne, 1991). The choice of the three towns (Hamnett, 1991), and the appropriateness of examining free-standing towns when most of the British population live in connurbations (Byrne, 1991), has caused concern about how far Saunders' findings can be generalized. Also, Forrest and Murie (1990) have suggested that the way questions about satisfaction with housing were phrased would lead people to express satisfaction with owner-occupation and dissatisfaction with council housing. For example, tenants were asked 'Has there ever been any problem in your experience in getting the sort of council house you want in the place you want?' while owners were asked 'The price of housing has gone up a lot over the years. Would you say you have made money out of owning a house?' Forrest and Murie maintain that 'these are leading and loaded questions with problems of prestige bias' (1990, p.626).

(3) Forrest and Murie examined the questionnaire closely partly because Saunders reports much higher levels of dissatisfaction among council tenants than other comparable surveys. Previous research has suggested that 'many households with direct experience of both tenures have positive views of *both* home-ownership and council housing.' (Forrest and Murie, 1990; p.629)

Most critics contend that Saunders, because of his desire to make a strong distinction between state and market, has exaggerated the importance of differences in tenure (i.e. in the legal condition of owner-ship). It is not so much ownership as the comparative quality of houses that concerns people. Quality – size, amenities, garden, location, etc., – is what matters; people's judgments depend on how good public housing is when compared with other alternatives. Hence, Forrest and Murie claim that the research 'does not support a picture of tenure choice and preference deriving either from ideological pressures, a natural desire to own or preferences constructed around tenure itself' (1990, p.633).

For the same reason, Saunders tends to ignore differences in the quality of housing *within* different tenure categories. As more and more people become owners, the variation in their properties increases, with the cheapest owner-occupied property deteriorating and offering amenities considerably inferior to that on better council estates (see Forrest, Murie and Williams, 1990). Moreover, Saunders leaves out of consideration privately-rented accommodation, the least popular tenure of all (Harloe, 1992). This again demonstrates that market provision is not always good. Rather, it depends on the context and available alternatives what kind of provision gives preferred outcomes.

(4) Saunders showed that class position was more important than consumption location in explaining voting, but still, rightly, maintained that consumption opportunities were important. He stressed that because material wealth derived from owner-occupation working class people were no longer propertyless, and that, hence, class divisions were reduced.

Some critics have challenged his predictions about the effects of inheritance and capital gains on class inequalities. Several believe he mis-stated the process. The financial gain from owning poor standard houses is relatively limited. People with the most expensive houses, usually those in higher social classes, made far greater absolute gains than did working class people. If this were the case generally, housing markets would amplify, rather than counteract, class inequalities. However, regional differences in house prices make this a less than simple relationship.

Others have questioned whether the experience of the cohort investigated – which is the first generation of working class people to share in mass owner-occupation – will be repeated in subsequent decades. In the past most young couples began their housing careers as council tenants and saved for a mortgage. If public sector housing stock declines in number and quality, the process of transition to owner-occupation may alter. If access to home-ownership becomes dependent upon family support, class divisions may easily reassert themselves. Probably more depends on the supply of new dwellings than Saunders recognises, for he focused exclusively on demand.

(5) The general argument about the deteriorating circumstances of tenants in public housing, a process sometimes described by others as 'socio-tenurial polarization' (Hamnett, 1984), seems firmly established. As the best council property is sold off, and as those who can afford it buy into the owner-occupied sector, the residents remaining on council estates tend to be the poor and the elderly. Under present housing policies, a vicious cycle of deteriorating conditions is the most likely outcome. Critics, however, refuse to describe this in terms of the emergence of an 'underclass', people dependant, across the board, on state support. The objection is partly political, but also conceptual: most commentators find the notion inapplicable as a way of understanding poverty and deprivation in the UK (e.g. Bagguley and Mann, 1992; Morris and Irwin, 1992). Moreover, as Saunders uses the term, it suggests a return to diagnosis in terms of consumption cleavages, which position he had apparently abandoned after examining the data about voting. People's housing conditions depend on a number of factors – class, income, age, region, gender and local area. The concept of polarization fails to capture the intricacies of the distributive aspects of housing.

Conclusion

A Nation of Home Owners is a contentious book, but one which explores in depth important issues regarding the social, pyschological and political significance of housing. The acceptability of its most general conclusions probably depends more on the political convictions of the reader than on the balance of the sociological argumentation. The empirical research itself perhaps needs repetition, using a larger sample of respondents in different places, to confirm its validity. Nevertheless, it is probably safe to say that buying a house has been a good financial investment for most people and that home owners do not live especially privatized lifestyles. Also, consumption cleavages are neither independent of, nor have they replaced, class divisions, though there is currently an increasing concentration of poorer and older people in council housing. Moreover, Saunders is correct to suggest that in the field of housing, state policy, regarding tax-relief to homeowners and restrictions on local authority building pro- grammes, is central in determining satisfaction for most people.

Bibliography

Bagguley, P. and Mann, K. (1992), 'Idle thieving bastards: scholarly representations of the underclass' in *Work Employment and Society*, Vol.6, No.1, (1992), pp.113–126.

Byrne, D. (1991), Review article in *International Journal of Urban and Regional Research*, Vol.15, No.4, pp.633–638.

Dunleavy, P. (1980), *Urban Political Analysis: the politics of collective consumption*, London, Macmillan.

Edgell, S. and Duke, V. (1991), *A Measure of Thatcherism: a sociology of Britain*, London, Harper Collins.

Forrest, R. (1991), Review of 'A Nation of Home Owners' in *Progress in Human Geography*, Vol.15, pp.366–369.

Forrest, R. and Murie, A. (1990), 'A dissatisfied state?: consumer preferences and council housing in Britain' in *Urban Studies*, Vol.27, No.5, pp.617–635.

Forrest, R., Murie, A. and Williams, P. (1990), *Home Ownership: differentiation and fragmentation*, London, Unwin Hyman.

Hamnett, C. (1984), 'Housing the two nations: socio-tenurial polarisa- tion in England and Wales, 1961–81' in *Urban Studies*, Vol.21, No.4, pp.389–405.

Hamnett, C. (1991), Review of 'A Nation of Home Owners' in *Sociology*, Vol.25, No.1, pp.133–4.

Harloe, M. (1992), Review of 'A Nation of Home Owners', in *Environ- ment and Planning D: Society and Space*, Vol.10, No.1, pp.99–102.

Morris, L. and Irwin, S. (1992), 'Employment histories and the concept of the underclass' in *Sociology*, Vol.26, No.3, pp.401–420.

Saunders, P. (1986), *Social Theory and the Urban Question*, (2nd edition) London, Hutchinson.

Saunders, P. (1990), *A Nation of Home Owners*, London, Unwin Hyman.

Appendices

Table 5.1 Reasons for first house purchase

| | Town | | | | | | | |
| | Burnley | | Derby | | Slough | | Total | |
Reason for buying	No.	%	No.	%	No.	%	No.	%
Get something for your money	31	27	39	32	34	27	104	29
Investment	31	27	16	13	26	21	73	20
Desire to own	17	15	25	21	21	17	63	18
No choice	15	13	14	12	34	27	63	18
Automatic, parents own, etc.	16	14	11	9	11	9	38	11
Could afford it so bought	4	4	12	10	14	11	30	8
Security	6	5	12	10	9	7	27	8
Autonomy, independence	7	4	7	6	11	9	25	7
Other reasons	29	26	36	30	45	36	110	31

Total number of respondents = 359 (Burnley 113, Derby 121, Slough 125)

(Saunders, 1990, Table 2.3, p.85)

Table 5.2 Perceived advantages and disadvantages of council house renting

| | Town | | | | | | | |
| | Burnley | | Derby | | Slough | | Total | |
	No.	%	No.	%	No.	%	No.	%
Perceived advantages								
No advantages	16	36	17	36	21	57	54	42
Get repairs done	15	34	13	28	9	26	37	29
Cheaper than buying	4	9	5	11	5	14	15	12
Others	10	22	11	24	5	14	26	21
Don't know	3	7	2	4	2	6	7	6
Perceived disadvantages								
Lack of personal control	6	15	13	29	8	26	27	24
Money down the drain	5	12	6	13	14	45	25	21
No disadvantages	10	24	13	29	1	3	24	20
Repairs don't get done	6	15	7	16	6	19	19	17
More expensive than buying	6	15	2	4	4	13	12	10
Others	13	32	10	22	9	29	32	27
Don't know	2	5	3	7	2	7	7	6

Total number of respondents = 125 (advantages), 118 (disadvantages)

(ibid., Table 2.5, p.89)

Table 5.3 Housing tenure and neighbourhood relations

	Housing tenure			
	Home owners		Council tenants	
Neighbourhood relations	No.	%	No.	%
At least one close friend living in the neighbourhood	89	35	56	56
At least one close friend living in the town	112	44	57	57
At least one close friend met through the neighbourhood	82	35	44	50
At least one close friend known since childhood	71	31	77	90
Has lived in three or more dwellings since first set up home	182	50	60	46
Always lived in the same town since first set up home	205	56	101	79
Thinks neighbourhood is friendly or very friendly	216	60	77	60
No favours or aid for or from neighbours	100	29	37	30
Regular help by or for neighbours	38	11	23	19

Note: Totals differ for each item due to missing data.
(ibid., Table 5.5, p.285)

6

Working in Catering

Yannis Gabriel (1988), *Working Lives in Catering*, London, Routledge

Roger Walters

The Sociology of the Catering Service

'You serve hundreds of people here each day . . . But most of them hardly seem to notice you – all they want is to get served as soon as possible and that's all that matters. Sometimes I think that this uniform makes me invisible.'

'It's all artificial. Pretending to offer personal service with a smile when in reality no one means it. We know this, management know this, even the customers know this, but we keep pretending. All they want to do is to take the customer's money as soon as possible. This is what it's all designed to achieve.'

(Fast-food workers, Gabriel, 1988, pp.3 and 93).

Recently there has been increasing interest in the changing nature of work; in the decline of the 'traditional' sectors of industry along with the growth in the areas of service and information. This interest relates to the *structure* of work. There has also been interest in examining the effects that this has had on workers – both inside and outside the labour market. The latter concern relates to the *meaning* of work. Nevertheless, certain sectors of the service industry, notably catering, have received little attention from sociologists.

Gabriel's research is therefore a welcome departure. It documents what he refers to as a 'revolution' in our eating and drinking habits and tastes. Now, what we eat, where we eat and how we eat, have changed so significantly that past generations may well have difficulty recognising aspects of these habits. Doubtless they would be surprised, if not amused and annoyed, by take-away meals, fast-food, health-food, wine bars, *haute cuisine* restaurants, and ethnic cafes and restaurants. Gabriel focuses on some of the workers providing meals in certain establishments, including hospitals and community centres. As he points out, they are an army of the low paid. They are also invisible, as the fast-food worker, quoted above, maintains. This is because, as customers, we are often too concerned with the food itself to notice who has served it, and this is especially the case with 'fast food'. Moreover, generally, those who have prepared and cooked it are well hidden behind closed doors. Gabriel also shows that catering workers are at the bottom of the wages league in the mid-1980s. He compares the average hourly pay for all full-time male workers of £3.19 with that of most male workers in his sample who received less than £2 per hour. A comparison between these and female rates of pay, both inside and outside catering, would have proved even more disparate, I suspect. Yet, as Gabriel further demonstrates, pay and visibility are part of a range of problems experienced by catering workers.

Intellectual Context

Gabriel's research examines six differing catering environments – a traditional mass catering unit in a hospital, a modern frozen-food unit in a community centre, three outlets of a fast-food chain, a gentleman's club, a traditional fish and chips restaurant, and a kebab house. His study relates to the sociology of work, industry and occupations in three ways.

First, it contributes to debates on the shift of work to an expanding tertiary or service sector of society. As employment in the manufacturing sector declined, Daniel Bell predicted a massive economic and social transformation to a 'post-industrial' service society (Bell, 1976). Thus, as Rosemary Crompton notes, it is the fact that the McDonalds hamburger chain employs more people than the steel industry that most people remember (Crompton, 1989). Gabriel suggests that this process may be called the 'McDonaldization of the economy'. Its significance was perhaps even more clearly seen by Charles Handy who noted that the *increase* in employment in eating and drinking places since 1973 is *greater* than *total* employment in the automobile *and* steel industries *combined* (Handy, 1984).

Second, the study of catering as a 'critical' case in the service sector reflects its rapidly changing nature. In examining various aspects of this work, Gabriel shows catering was once a traditional 'craft' industry, a 'people's industry' dependant for its success upon the social and technical skills of its personnel, together with their ingenuity, hard work, commitment and 'attitude'. It has been transformed into modern catering, exemplified by the range and complexity of its technical hardware, the meticulous planning, standardization and marketing of its products and services and the fragmentation of its production techniques. The change was most apparent in the survival of 'craft' skills in catering at the hospital and gentleman's club –

'home-cooking writ large' – as distinct from the sophisticated catering hardware in use at the community centre and the convenience-food being served at the fast-food outlets. Planning and technology have come to replace the 'human factor', whether it be the cook's artistry, the waiter's manners or the manager's conviviality.

Third, Gabriel examines catering from within the context of the labour process debate. The labour process is a term usually associated with manufacturing and production. It refers to the means by which raw materials are transformed by human labour, using tools and machinery, first into products for use, and, under capitalism, into commodities to be exchanged on the market. Key issues here include the management and control of production and of labour, technology, the de-skilling and degradation of work and alienation at work. Gabriel relates these to the changing nature of catering work. Catering is now characterized by the highly technological, fragmented and routinized production of standardized products in which the workforce is carefully managed. What, asks Gabriel, are the implications of such changes on the work and working conditions of those occupied in the catering service? Have catering workers been liberated from the drudgery of boring, repetitive and arduous work? Are they now allowed to use their skills and intelligence, or does the new catering technology exacerbate feelings of powerlessness and meaninglessness by turning workers into 'ever less significant cogs of vast production machines?' Do mechanisms still exist for effective labour resistance?

Research Design

There are, in *Working Lives in Catering*, six case studies of some 200 workers in different establishments. Gabriel's purpose was to provide a realistic picture of the working lives and outlooks of catering workers and management. The studies exemplify the vast complexity of the catering industry whilst reflecting the transition from traditional to modern techniques.

Saint Theresa's, a teaching hospital in the heart of London, has a traditional mass-catering unit; Michael Lansby, a community centre in the outskirts of a large northern city is the location of a modern frozen-food unit providing meals for two comprehensive schools and six other schools, an old-age pensioners luncheon club, a meals-on-wheels service, an adult education and two further education canteens, four snack bars and a staff-social dining room; Saint George's is a business-men's club in a large Midland city in which the catering service provides traditional English cooking; three London outlets of a fast-food chain, Fun Food International, testified to the 'catering revolution', whilst the small independent sector was represented by a traditional fish and chips restaurant and a kebab house.

In order to portray what Gabriel calls 'the vast collage of human histories' at St Theresa's, he use a combination of informal interviews and conversations, complemented by more structured interviews. This procedure was repeated elsewhere to varying extents, the workers ranging from unskilled teenagers at Fun Foods, to married women at the community centre and the gentleman's club and to middle-aged and elderly Spanish, West Indian, Italian and Portuguese immigrants at the hospital. Gabriel also drew on the catering experiences, in fast-food outlets, of 25 of his students. Their responses illustrated and amplified some of the points made by other respondents.

The aim was to obtain an idea of the depth, and strength, of feeling of catering workers about their job. To this end Gabriel constructed an interview schedule of 85 questions, some with supplementaries. From this seemingly ambitious programme Gabriel was able to produce statistical tables on, amongst other issues, workers attitudes toward management, unions, length of service, work priorities, job evaluation and interest in the job. Using this schedule Gabriel conducted 59 structured interviews, from a total staff of 88, at St Theresa's; 57, from 70, at Michael Lansby and 48 at the 'fun food machines'.

Principal Findings

There are four specific and inter-related findings.

First, the study indicates the diversity of the catering industry. Gabriel found differences between and within catering organizations. He examined a broad spectrum of concerns – both large and small, private and public, technologically advanced or otherwise together with both individual and mass-catering. The range of workers was diverse – older, 'trapped' immigrant workers; younger, qualified, skilled cooks; married women, combining occupational labour with domestic labour; teenage workers, seeing work as a 'brief interlude'; and business owners doing arduous work for long hours as the price of independence. Yet within the organizations there were also differences – between the traditional craft skills of the cooks, and the routine work of dining-room staff at the hospital; between mass-catering hardware at the cook-freeze centre in the community centre and one of the cooks in the Further Education canteen at the centre who 'produced' her own cooking. Her curries and vegetarian dishes were especially popular among Asian students.

Second, Gabriel discusses the implications of changes in catering on the work and working conditions of catering workers. The new catering technology at Michael Lansby community centre represented Taylorist principles in mass-catering. The cook-freeze kitchen, which supplied meals to institutions within and outside the centre, exempli-fied the application of factory production in catering. The product, the meal to be preserved in ice in large freezers, was simple and uniform, cooked in large quantities in distinct stages with each worker carrying out a different task. Cooking was thus split up from planning, work tasks were broken up into simple and tightly controlled routines, skill was reduced, and the initiative and thinking required by the cooks was minimal. This represented a deskilling, mechanization and standardization of the catering industry, as forecast by Braverman's analysis of the service sector. It also represents the characteristics of 'Fordism' that Braverman argued were developing in the late 20th century. Thus, it could be argued from Gabriel's work, that elements of Fordism, in which catering work is mechanized, routinized, closely supervized and de-skilled, were extant in Britain during the 1980s. In contrast, some sociologists of work have identified a transition away from Fordism to a more flexible system of production – neo or post-Fordism (see Wood, 1989).

Gabriel also examines changes arising from the closer supervision of work tasks at St Theresa's hospital. 'The changes', as the workers at the hospital called them, were part of a new rigorous system of work imposed by management. They were instigated in the context of government moves toward privatization. Such changes involved 'flexible work arrangements', with mobility of staff from section to section, new job descriptions which removed traditional lines of demarcation and a new rostering system which dramatically reduced the amount of staff overtime. This stricter control and organization of the work by management proved a source of dissatisfaction and stress for workers, leading to a sharp division between them and management. Nevertheless, some workers were less dissatisfied – the cooks, whose traditional craft had been preserved, and the managers themselves, who were in a position of greater control.

Third, Gabriel examines how catering workers felt in response to changes in the technology and management of catering services. The predominant feeling was of being trapped in the job, a feeling of powerlessness in which their lives were perceived as meaningless. From this the realities of the workplace were, for Gabriel, 'intimately connected' with social and economic depression and the government's handling of it. Generally, dissatisfying characteristics of catering work included routine, repetitive and boring jobs; problems of living on a low rate of pay; feelings of fear and insecurity; a sense of the close supervision of their work as management asserted their right to manage. For example, married women at the community centre were tied to their jobs due to family obligations, in some cases as the sole breadwinner, in others as dual worker families. Moreover, the specific 'changes' at the hospital had brought absenteeism and bitterness. Even the cooks, who were not as dissatisfied as other catering workers, had considered the possibility of moving to another job sooner or later. Workers were divided by skill, age, nationality and by management. Indeed, only three groups of workers found their work instrinsically satisfying or challenging – the hospital cooks, the staff serving in the small dining areas at the community centre and the staff in the gentleman's club. The feature of the work situation of all these groups was freedom from interference. Yet the common denominator of low wages, routine work and pressure at work was apparent – 'needing the money means needing the job'.

Fourth, Gabriel concludes that, on the basis of his research, class distinctions in British society are neither being blurred nor obliterated by the development of a service economy and by mass unemployment. Furthermore, he argues, workers have not lost the will to resist the power of capital. Whilst mass production techniques in catering have led to significant profits for some capitalists, catering workers resisted, albeit in small ways. A milk bottle with a couple of flowers, a transistor radio blaring at all times, a painting on the wall done by 'one of the lads' were attempts to influence the work environment. This daily contestation of the work terrain is a relatively weak form of worker resistance symptomatic of the political, economic and social context prevalent in the mid-1980s.

Methodology

Several important issues are raised by Gabriel's research. Apart from general issues relating to access, choice of the samples and the collection and recording of data, questions concerning the nature of *ethnography* are also relevant since this is the approach mainly utilized by Gabriel.

In some of the establishments Gabriel visited he was able quickly to gain the confidence of respondents. This was especially the case in the hospital, where many of the catering staff were foreign immigrants who had been working there for about 25 years. Gabriel was himself an immigrant and the catering staff treated him very generously, losing their inhibitions, and, because he was not seen to be part of the British class structure, providing information he might not otherwise have obtained.

Gabriel provides a brief rationale for his choice of the sample case studies. His aim was to select a range of establishments exemplifying traditional and modern catering, and both large bureaucratic, and small-scale, organizations. Are his chosen cases representative? Gabriel did cease to look for a representative sample of a '*haute cuisine*' restaurant since those he saw varied so much that there seemed little justification in concentrating on any of them. It may not be safe to assume then that the establishments Gabriel did select were representative.

Gabriel used structured and unstructured interviews to collect data. However, he did not tape-record them, preferring to record replies in note form. Gabriel found that it proved difficult to record quotes *verbatim* because his interview schedule of over ninety questions was wide ranging and possibly too ambitious for notation recording. Additionally, Gabriel was aware of the problem of finding methods which elicit and record information that encompasses the varied range and complexity of human experience. For example, when catering workers from different cultures responded differently to the same interview questions, as happened at the hospital, Gabriel was unsure whether this was due to genuine differences in their experiences or whether it reflected differences in expression and communication.

Some of these issues and problems relate specifically to the ethnographic approach taken by Gabriel. Because he examines only a few case studies it is difficult for him to make generalizations. Also, since he is not using experimental manipulation and quantitative measurement of variables, he is unable rigorously to test explanatory hypotheses. However, Gabriel may well argue that in describing and understanding the way of life and the naturally occurring behaviour of these catering workers, he is more concerned with exploring the nature of social phenomena, with discovering their character, rather than limiting himself to the testing of explicit hypotheses, whilst seeking to make generalizations.

Evaluation

Rosemary Crompton (1989) makes one general and two particular criticisms of Gabriel's work.

Generally, she maintains that his theoretical perspectives within industrial sociology are not always made absolutely clear. What she seems to be saying is that Gabriel has insufficiently related his research on catering workers to the major debates on work orientation, deskilling and the impact of technology.

In particular, Crompton maintains that Gabriel presents no systematic discussion of theories of labour market segmentation, or feminist theories, both of which, arguably, would have made a useful contribution to the interpretation of his valuable research material. Segmented labour markets mean the division of the workforce by patterns of institutionalized discrimination – race and gender are powerful sources of differentiation. Developing Crompton's critique it could be argued that Gabriel presents little evidence, and therefore explanation, of inequalities between women and men in the catering service. For instance, are the higher paid cooks and 'master chefs' predominantly male? Clearly this is beyond the boundaries of this research, yet Gabriel does perhaps pay insufficient attention to catering as a gendered occupation. He does not, for example, provide detailed evidence of the predominance of women in the lower echelons of the hierarchy of catering workers, and of the ideology whereby their work is seen as an extension of the duties of a housewife who prepares, cooks and serves family meals.

The second specific criticism is made by Crompton when she draws attention to an empirical gap in the research, and this is the absence of any data from the hotel or restaurant trade. This is an ommission that Gabriel acknowledges. It is, Crompton argues, possible that 'attitudes to work' might be rather different in this sector. We may apply the same point to other catering outlets, including Chinese and Indian take-aways, *haute cuisine* restaurants, sandwich bars, public houses serving food and so on. Therefore, although Gabriel tries to cover the complex and various world of catering through examining six case studies, he still fails fully to reflect the diversity of this industry.

Of course the danger in doing more, in filling this 'gap', over and above the problem of representativeness, is that the research becomes too superficial.

Conclusion

Gabriel's research is an excellent example of an ethnographic study and a welcome addition to an aspect of service work lacking empirical studies. The diversity of catering establishments covered is very good for such a relatively short study. They include a hospital, community centre, fast-food outlets, a private club, a restaurant serving fish and chips and a kebab house. Variation between the situations themselves and between workers at these establishments, together with the wide range of catering styles from traditional catering for small, and larger, groups, to modern, technological catering methods, evidences Gabriel's hard work. Moreover, it is written in a clear and coherent style, and is an absorbing and interesting read, even for those for whom catering and culinary concerns are, if anything, limited to domestic matters!

In examining catering from within the context of change, continuity and control, Gabriel's research is an account of workplace relations in Britain clearly exemplifying debates on the labour process including the work of Taylor, Bell, Braverman, and, more recently, Wood and Thompson. One aspect concerns the effect of technology on catering workers. There is, Gabriel concludes, no iron law here. Technology does not necessarily dictate either work experience or the work itself, nor does it 'cause' alienation. In fast-food, for example, perhaps of all the case studies the most significantly influenced by technology, Gabriel found considerable differences amongst the three outlets. This related to how much people talk to each other, the informality, or otherwise, of their relationships, the quality of the product and the speed of work.

Finally, this is an interesting and in some ways an entertaining book, but it is also challenging. Amidst social and economic depression, it provides a voice for some of the most vulnerable and exploited sections of the working class – married women, foreign workers, part-time, teenage and unskilled workers – whose 'discontents mirror the hidden injuries of class of many generations of workers who have reluctantly sold their labour power to capital' (Gabriel, 1988, pp.167–8). Yet Gabriel also traces how capital has fought back, how managers have got tough and re-asserted their right to manage, how tasks have been better organized (in other words greater control of the work process) so that companies are more successful, and how significant profits are being made by the application of techniques of mass production derived from manufacturing. The 'tragedy' experienced by catering workers is low wages, boring work, poor working conditions, arrogant management and a lack of control over forces which dominate their lives. But they are trapped because they depend on capital for their livelihood. Out of this deep ambivalence catering workers are fighting back in small but significant ways, Gabriel argues. Ultimately however, what he describes is a politics of confrontation which has deepened the divide between workers and management in which the job of the latter is to keep the lid on the workers' discontents. Consequently, this is not a book to generate optimistism in the re-birth of a post-industrialist era of new industrial relations. Nevertheless, in seeking for solutions we need first to understand the problem. Reading Gabriel will certainly help us to do this.

Bibliography

Bell, D. (1976), *The Coming of Post-Industrial Society*, Harmondsworth, Penguin.

Braverman, H. (1974), *Labor and Monopoly Capital*, New York, Monthly Review Press.

Crompton, R. (1989), Review of 'Working Lives in Catering' in *Work, Employment and Society*, Vol. 3, No. 1, pp.129–130.

Hammersley, M. (1990), *Reading Ethnographic Research: A Critical Guide*, Harlow, Longman.

Hammersley, M. (1992), 'Introducing Ethnography' in *Sociology Review*, Vol. 2, No. 2, pp.18–23.

Handy, C. (1984), *The Future of Work*, Oxford, Blackwell.

McNeill, P. (1985), *Research Methods*, (especially Ch. 4), London, Tavistock.

Thompson, P. (1989), *The Nature of Work*, Basingstoke, Macmillan,

Warde, A. (1989), 'The Future of Work' in *Social Studies Review*, Vol. 5, No. 1, pp.11–15.

Wood, S. (ed.) (1982), *The Degradation of Work? Skill, De-skilling and the Labour Process*, London, Hutchinson.

Wood, S. (ed.) (1989), *The Transformation of Work: skill, flexibility and the labour process*, (especially the introduction), London, Unwin Hyman.

Appendices

Table 6.1 Staff attitudes towards management

	ST*			ML†					FF‡		
	C	P	D	CF	P	FE	SM	D	M	SU	S
The manager											
friendly, informal	12	5	7	4	0	2	5	13	12	2	19
formal, impersonal	1	2	1	9	3	7	1	9	2	3	6
correct but unfriendly	3	6	1	3	0	5	2	9			
pushy, bossy	3	4	8	1	0	1	0	1	0	1	4
lackadaisical									1	0	0
two-faced									0	1	1
TOTAL	19	17	17	17	3	15	8	32	15	7	30
Management											
doing a good job	13	8	6	3	1	0	3	5	12	3	15
a good job for themselves/the store but bad for staff				3	0	5	1	7	1	0	5
not doing a good job	4	6	8	10	2	9	3	15	1	1	4
don't know/so-so	2	3	3	1	0	1	1	5	1	3	2
TOTAL	19	17	17	17	3	15	8	32	15	7	26
Managers are arrogant to staff											
disagree	13	10	8	2	2	2	3	7	15	3	11
agree	3	6	9	13	1	13	4	22	0	4	13
don't know	3	1	0	2	0	0	1	3	0	0	2
TOTAL	19	17	17	17	3	15	8	32	15	7	26

* ST St Theresa's
  C: Cooks (all grades)
  P: Kitchen and Trolley Porters
  D: Dining-room staff including supervisors

† ML Michael Lansby
  CF: Cook-freeze kitchen staff
  P: Porters
  FE: Further education and OAP dining-room staff
  SM: School-meals staff
  D: All dining-room staff

‡ FF 3 Fast Food Stores
  M: Management
  SU: Supervisors
  S: Staff

(Gabriel, 1988, compiled from Table 1.10, p.43, Table 2.9, p.79, Table 3.9, p.117)

Passage 62:
Work satisfaction varied between establishments, as the following comments show. The first two relate to 'craft' cooking at St. Theresa's, the next three exhibit a far more instrumental attitude reflecting the more modern technology of the catering process at Michael Lansby.

'I love this hospital. I like cooking *for patients*. Everyone works for money but it is not enough.'
(Barbara, an assistant head cook, ibid., p.27)

'I love the job! There is variety, it's interesting. I enjoy doing it, that's what keeps me here.'
(Nick, a young trainee cook, ibid., p.27)

'This is not really catering, more like working in a factory. The product is irrelevant, it's not like cooking at home – you just have to do everything by the book, the same day in day out. There is much less variety now, we used to do more different dishes.'
(Norma Collins, the cook-freeze kitchen, ibid., p.66)

'My job is important for me, for the money and to get out of the home. At the moment there are no other jobs I could do, with the children. But when they grow up I would like to get a more interesting job, textiles designing perhaps or clerical. I would like a job with responsibility, to feel that people depended on me.'
(Moira, 30, mother of three children, had been working at Michael Lansby for three years, ibid., p.69)

'I would rather work part-time, that would be fairer to the family, wouldn't it. But we need the money, especially now that my husband has lost his job. This is why I am trying to make a go of it here.'
(Vivien Morris, the cook-freeze kitchen, ibid., p.69)

7

Gender Relations at Work in Britain

Rosemary Crompton and Kay Sanderson (1991), *Gendered Jobs and Social Change*, London, Unwin Hyman.

Dawn Burton

Women and Work

An increase in women's employment has been a persistent feature of many Western societies for the last 30 years. The sex-typing of particular occupations as men's and women's work is also an observable feature of most societies. An important objective for sociologists, is to try and identify factors which provide an explanation for occupational segregation within the workplace.

Hakim (1979) has suggested that gender segregation within paid employment needs to be considered in terms of both horizontal, and vertical segregation. Horizontal segregation exists where men and women work in different occupations. For example, women tend to be concentrated in clerical work and personal services, such as catering, cleaning and hairdressing. Men, on the other hand, predominate in the traditional craft occupations such as those in the building, and engineering industry. Vertical segregation occurs when men and women work within the same industry, but men occupy the high level, high status, and women the low level, low status, positions. For example, whilst large numbers of women are infant and primary school teachers, most of the heads of those schools are men.

A number of theoretical explanations have been advanced by sociologists to account for gender segregation within the workplace. These can be divided into those which focus on the qualities of female labour, and others which emphasise labour market segmentation and other institutional factors. Both sex-role theory and human capital theory stress the qualities of female labour. Sex-role theorists highlight the importance of socio-cultural factors by arguing that women are socialised from an early age to discern the difference between male and female occupations. They draw attention to the fact that much of the paid work women perform outside the home, such as cooking, cleaning and caring tasks, resembles tasks undertaken within the household. According to this perspective, the perceived qualities of female labour account for the occupational segregation in employment. By contrast, human capital theorists argue that women have failed to invest sufficiently in their 'human capital', such as gaining formal qualifications, acquiring training and having an unbroken service record. They suggest that these activities have not been given a high priority by women, whose ultimate aim is to leave work to have a family. As a result of this lack of investment, many women are only qualified to be employed a narrow range of relatively unskilled occupations.

Explanations which focus on labour market segmentation and institutional factors include dual labour market theory and patriarchy. Dual labour market theorists stress the significance of labour market segmentation. They argue that women are viewed as secondary workers by employers, whilst men occupy positions in the primary workforce. Employers perceive women to be less career orientated than men because of their family responsibilities. Women are also often viewed by employers as reluctant to seek higher monetary rewards, or training. Employers' perceptions of women employees would therefore explain why so many women occupy the lower level occupations within organizational hierarchies. A further explanation, the theory of patriarchy, has been developed by feminists to emphasise the oppressive and exploitative nature of gender relations in society. They argue that the reason why women are concentrated in a narrow range of occupations and in low status positions, is because men, sometimes organized within trade unions, have excluded women from high status, well-paid work.

In *Gendered Jobs and Social Change*, Crompton and Sanderson discuss how gender relations in four areas of employment in Britain, those of pharmacy, accountancy, building societies and cooking and serving in hotel and catering and the school meal service, have changed over time. They argue that occupational segregation needs to be explained differently within each industry. Nevertheless, a number of themes are present: the acquisition of qualifications which enable women to gain access to management positions; difficulties women face because of male exclusionary tactics; problems associated with fulfilling geographical mobility and shift work; and cultural definitions of 'women's work'.

The main objective of the book is to analyse the changing nature of gender relations in the workplace. However, the authors argue that the issue of occupational segregation should be set within the context of other important social changes which have occurred in Britain since World War Two. In particular, they highlight the increasing acceptability of women undertaking paid work outside the home, rather than being a full-time housewife and mother. There are many more educational opportunities available to women, which have enabled them to enter a wider range of occupations. Equal opportunities legislation has also been a positive move, by the state, to encourage women to compete with men on a more equal footing and employers have been keen to attract women back into the workforce, and have constructed part-time employment opportunities to enable them to work around their domestic responsibilities. Whilst occupational segregation is an important area of sociological investigation in its own right, it nevertheless impinges on other areas of the sociology curriculum. These include debates surrounding the *domestic divisions of labour*, the *sociology of education*, and *gender relations in society*.

Research Design

The research on which the book is based was originally undertaken as three different projects between 1984 and 1988. The results of seven lengthy interviews with professionally qualified women pharmacists and six qualified accountants are discussed. The interviews were taped and then transcribed *verbatim*. Because the numbers in the samples were small, women were not randomly selected. Rather, the researchers selected women whom they considered representative of others in that occupation or profession.

A range of research sources was used in the case studies of gender segregation in building societies. Altogether, data were collected from three building societies; one very large, one large and one small society. To preserve the anonymity of the three organizations they were given fictional names, the 'Cloister', the 'Holyoake Permanent' and the 'Regional Plus' respectively. A total of eight managerial and 24 clerical and supervisory interviews were undertaken. Two building societies also provided documentary evidence, such as the numbers of men and women who were employed and at what level in the organizational hierarchy. The Building Societies Association and the Chartered Building Societies Institute also provided data about employment patterns throughout the industry.

The case study of the school meals service took place in a single education authority. Interviews were carried out with the head of the service, two school meals organizers and a trade union representative. Women working in the kitchen of a large comprehensive school were also interviewed. Brief life-history details were collected and longer, unstructured interviews were undertaken with the cook and cook-supervisor. The case study of the hotel and catering sector was undertaken in two hotels. A range of staff were interviewed from waitresses to a Personnel Manager. However, the numbers of respondents were not disclosed, neither were any details about the form, or duration of these interviews.

Principal Findings

(i) *Qualifications and occupations: the example of pharmacy*

Crompton and Sanderson indicate that pharmacy is an occupation which has been gradually feminising since World War Two. In the

1940s and 1950s female members of the profession increased by 5% a decade, by comparison with 10% in the 1970s and 1980s (*Table 7.1*, p.81). In 1983, 62% of University places and 51% of Polytechnic places for studying pharmacy, went to women. Pharmacy has not traditionally been sex-typed because of the high level of rigorous scientific training required to qualify. However, it has been an attractive occupation for women to enter because of the flexibility it offers. The women interviewed by Crompton and Sanderson stressed the extensive availability of part-time work in community, or retail, pharmacy.

On qualifying, pharmacists have a choice of three long-term career routes; as a pharmacist in the National Health Service (NHS), an owner or employee in an independently owned pharmacy, or as a manager/practitioner in a large company such as Boots. Despite the opportunity of three distinct career paths, Crompton and Sanderson demonstrate that women pharmacists are overwhelmingly located in the NHS. This feature is attributed to the image of the NHS as employer of caring professionals. This is in sharp contrast to the perceived characteristics of community pharmacy which included toughness, entrepreneurship, and the need for capital to set up a business. Moreover, women pharmacists in the NHS are usually concentrated in the lowest grades, leaving the internal labour market (the career ladder *within* the organization) open for men. In the case of pharmacy, the entry of women into the profession has not upset prevailing gender relations.

Pharmacy is an occupation where men and women are equal as far as qualifications are concerned. However, the need to combine domesticity with near continuous employment serves to reproduce the gender order, whereby women are subordinate to men within the profession.

(ii) *Qualifications, occupations and organizations:*
    the example of accountancy

Unlike pharmacy, which has been slowly feminised since the 1940s, the active recruitment of women to accountancy only occurred in the mid-1970s. Up until the mid-1960s women accounted for less than 1% of the membership of the Institute of Chartered Accountants in England and Wales (ICAEW). However, in 1987, 39% of ICAEW members, in the age range 23–26, were women. On qualifying, accountants have the choice of being employed in a large organization, perhaps in the accountancy department, or some other area of management. In this instance Crompton and Sanderson state that accountants will have organizational careers and use the firms internal labour market to gain promotion. The alternative choice would be for accountants to work, perhaps on a self-employed basis, in a small accountancy practice and here Crompton and Sanderson believe that accountants have occupational, rather than organizational, careers because they earn their living from being accountants, and because there are few possibilities for promotion in small practices. The authors argue that women who pursue organizational careers by using the firms' internal labour market are more prone to discriminatory practices because they are competing directly with men for promotion. This situation rarely confronts women who choose the practitioner option.

During the research Crompton and Sanderson interviewed women accountants who worked in large organizations. They vividly described their experiences of male discriminatory practices. However, they also indicated the capacity to resist such discrimination (see *Passage 7.1*, p.82). Crompton and Sanderson conclude that women who have qualified as accountants in an era of greater gender equality, are better placed to resist sexual discrimination than women who qualified at a time when 'gender exclusion was legally and socially acceptable' (Crompton and Sanderson, 1991, p.103).

Unlike the situation in pharmacy, where part-time work was freely available, part-time work in accountancy was usually only available in small accountancy practices. Organizational careers did not easily facilitate the dual role of mother and professional employee. It was a generally held view by the women interviewed that organizational careers came to an end with the onset of part-time employment. Consequently, young women accountants faced the choice; children or career.

(iii) *Organizations and their labour markets:*
    the building society industry

Unlike accountancy, employment within building societies has been extensively sex-typed as female. Crompton and Sanderson suggest that the primary reason is that building societies expanded at a time when there was a pool of well-educated women who wanted to work. At the Cloister Building Society 97% of clerical employees working in branch offices were women. Another reason why women predominate in the industry is because of the nature of the work. At the Holyoake Permanent and Regional Plus building societies women cashiers indicated that depositors liked a friendly, helpful service. Managers considered that women had the required combination of qualities and skills to provide a caring service to customers. The cashier-clerk position has, therefore, been defined as women's work which attracts few male applicants and little gender conflict. At the managerial level, however, gender conflict and discriminatory practices have been widespread.

Building society work did not provide extensive career opportunities for women. Few women achieved branch manager level, although a small number of women attained supervisory and assistant branch manager posts. In 1977 the reasons why women were not promoted to branch managerial posts became the subject of an Equal Opportunities Commission investigation. A Leeds Permanent Building Society job advertisement for trainee managers laid down three criteria for prospective candidates; those of age, qualifications and previous related work experience. The investigation found that women who possessed all three characteristics were less likely to be interviewed than men who had none of them. The Commission concluded that female applicants had been discriminated against because of their sex.

The EOC investigation was widely discussed within the building society industry. It was therefore highly likely that the ruling would have an impact on practices within the industry. Crompton and Sanderson's findings indicated that recruits for management training at the Cloister Building Society had been overwhelmingly male since the 1960s. However, from 1980 onwards this position was reversed (*Table 7.2*, p.82). To formalize its equal opportunities policy further, the Cloister Building Society made a decision that from 1990, promotions would not proceed without all applicants having the relevant qualifications.

(iv) *Women's work: cooking and serving*

Crompton and Sanderson's previous examples of women's employment focused on well-qualified women. Cooking and cleaning has, for the most part, been labelled as unskilled employment. This is largely because of its association with work undertaken within the home, which tends to be undervalued. The school meals service, for example, is dominated by women because the hours and holidays are suitable for women with young children at school. Employment in the school meals service has been labelled women's work and does not attract competition from men. For the most part, there are few opportunities for career advancement. However, it is possible to move from a kitchen assistant to be a cook-supervisor and from there to attain the highest position of assistant to the school meals organizer.

The hotel trade has also offered women flexible working hours which enable them to combine their responsibility for domestic labour with paid work. However, it appears that occupations in the hotel trade have not been stereotyped to the same extent as the school meals service. This is illustrated by Crompton and Sanderson's case study of two hotels which were owned by a regionally based company. In 1979 men were overwhelmingly concentrated in full-time jobs such as porters, managers and waiters. Women were overwhelmingly employed as part-time waitresses and chambermaids. By 1987, however, the proportion of men employed on a full-time basis in the two hotels had declined, whereas the proportion of women working full-time had risen. The number of male casual workers had also exhibited an increase. The reasons for the trends were explained by the company's Personnel Manager:

> We used to have more full-timers and permanents (i.e. part-timers) but as the need to make more profit becomes the greater you have to find a

way of making your workforce work for you rather than keeping it on all year. The computer can forecast trends more accurately, you can control your workforce by using casuals. Casuals can now work as much as full-timers. (ibid., p.149)

The need to reduce costs in the hotel industry had the effect of feminising some additional areas of work. A strategy of using more temporary workers, often students and other younger employees, was also used.

In commercial catering, especially in large hotels, women are under-represented at management level. The job requires extensive geographical mobility and the ability to work long shifts. Both conditions are difficult for women with domestic responsibilities to fulfil. Crompton and Sanderson also argue that women have been excluded from the traditional 'craft route' to management positions. Chefs, restaurant managers and wine waiters have traditionally been stereotyped as male occupations. It is significant that more women are choosing the qualifications route to management. In 1982/83 70% of students on higher level catering courses were women.

Throughout the book, Crompton and Sanderson demonstrate the complexity of occupational segregation in the workplace. They also provide evidence which indicates that recent social changes in Britain have produced an environment which has had a positive effect on women's employment opportunities. They note that it has become more socially acceptable for women to combine their domestic responsibilites with paid work. Many women are also making use of the 'qualifications lever' to increase their choice of occupations, and to reach managerial positions. In the building societies industry career routes, albeit restricted ones, have been designed with women in mind. Crompton and Sanderson also demonstrated the effect of recent equal opportunities legislation on occupational segregation within the workplace. In their case study of accountancy, women were able to compete on equal terms with men for promotion.

Critical Observations

Despite Crompton and Sanderson's contribution in unravelling the complex process of gender segregation, there are a number of ways in which their account should be critically assessed.

The fact that the book is based on a series of case studies raises issues about the generalizability of the findings (Bryman, 1989). Case studies are favoured by researchers because they provide a rich and detailed information source about the subject being researched. However, the issue of whether a particular organization or sample of subjects are representative of others, is a matter of considerable debate. One way of getting around this problem is to use several organizations in the same industry with different characteristics (such as size, number of employees and management structure) and then compare the results.

Crompton and Sanderson did this only in their research on the building society industry. The authors should have provided more details about their respondents. In some cases the reader does not know how many people have been interviewed, how those individuals were selected, where they were interviewed, or whether they were representative of others working in the occupation concerned.

Rothwell (1991) has also commented about the way in which the case studies in the book vary considerably, both in depth and breadth. Whilst some chapters are based on in-depth interviews and others on statistical data, others 'rely too much on anecdotal information'. This feature is reflected in the amount of secondary data (data collected by someone other than the researcher) used, which helps to disguise the fact that, at times, first hand accounts are a little thin on the ground.

Conclusion

Gendered Jobs and Social Change provides a useful contribution to existing explanations of occupational segregation in Britain. The strength of Crompton and Sanderson's argument is that they point to a range of social, cultural and political processes which shape the division of labour between men and women in particular occupations, rather than rely on one definitive theoretical framework. Their view that gender relations within occupations and industries do not take a single form, but are socially and historically constructed, requires and merits further research. Crompton and Sanderson also consider gender relations in occupations and industrial sectors which have often been neglected by sociologists. A great deal of industrial sociology has focused on manufacturing industry and skilled, male dominated occupations. Future research projects would need to explore the validity of Crompton and Sanderson's framework in a number of other occupations and industries. There is also scope for undertaking further research in the areas chosen by the authors, given the small size of their samples.

Bibliography and Further Reading

Bryman, A. (1988), *Doing Research in Organisations*, London, Routledge.

Bryman, A. (1989), *Research Methods and Organisation Studies*, London, Unwin Hyman.

Connell, R.W. (1987), *Gender and Power*, Cambridge, Polity.

Crompton, R. and Sanderson, K. (1991), *Gendered Jobs and Social Change*, London, Unwin Hyman.

Dex, S. (1991), Review of 'Gendered Jobs and Social Change' in *Industrial Relations Journal*, Vol. 22, No. 1, pp.75–77.

Hakim, C. (1979), 'Occupational Segregation', Research Paper No.9, November, London: Department of Employment.

Rothwell, S. (1991), Review of 'Gendered Jobs and Social Change' in *British Journal of Industrial Relations*, Vol. 29, No. 29, pp.355–356.

Walby, S. (ed.) (1988), *Gender Segregation at Work*, Milton Keyness, Open University Press.

Walby, S. (1986), *Patriarchy at Work*, Cambridges, Polity Press.

Appendices

Table 7.1 Men and Women in Pharmacy: selected years, by occupation

	1963 %		1972 %		1985 %	
	Men	Women	Men	Women	Men	Women
Community pharmacy	84	16	82	18	67	33
Hospital pharmacy	45	55	37	63	38	62
Industry	95	5	95	5	78	22
Other	82	18	77	23	76	24
Total	82	18	77	23	76	24

(adapted from Crompton and Sanderson, 1991, Table 4.1, p.76)

Passage 7.1:

A woman accountant recalling the discrimination at the hands of a male boss. (ibid., pp.103–104)

'I had a lot of problems with this boss. He was a professional chartered accountant, had trained in the profession, come in about seven years ago . . . eight or nine years now . . . but very insecure and he did a lot to try and undermine what I was trying to do in the department which I found impossible to deal with so, I think it was probably this time last year, I went to talk to Personnel and said, look, I need to talk to someone to get my side of it down on my Personnel file because I don't want to suddenly find that I've got black marks when I haven't had a chance to put my side of the story and I think, by then, I'd managed to establish a reputation – there weren't that many female accountants, and particularly not many female accountants who were very ambitious. The next thing I knew, I was being head-hunted by one of the general managers of one of the areas, discreetly taken out to lunch by somebody and then I was offered a job.'

Table 7.2 Cloister Building Society: recruitment of management trainees by gender

	Men		Women		Total	
	No.	%	No.	%	No.	%
1906–9*	158	93	12	7	170	100
1970–4†	199	98	5	2	204	100
1975–9	169	67	84	33	253	100
1980–5‡	30	35	57	65	87	100

Notes: * Data for 1961, 1962, 1963 not available
        † Data for 1972 not available
        ‡ Between 1980 and 1982 the Cloister virtually ceased recruitment of
          management trainees
(ibid., Table 6.1, p.119)

8

Women and the Professions

Anne Witz (1992), *Professions and Patriarchy*, London, Routledge.

Celia Lury

Introduction

It has long been recognized that women are under-represented in the professions. For example, over 80% of employers, managers and professionals were men in both 1971 and 1981, although the proportion of women did increase from 16% to 19% (Crompton and Sanderson, 1990). More concretely, in 1976, only 23% of all doctors on the General Medical Council were women; the situation had not substantially changed by the 1980s – only 13% of hospital consultants and 20% of principals in general practice are women (Allen, 1988). However, while these figures show the extent of gender inequality within the professions, they do not show *how* the professions have come to be gendered occupations.

In *Professions and Patriarchy*, Anne Witz puts forward a detailed historical analysis of the mechanisms through which professions have come to be gendered. She shows that men and women who take part in professional projects have had unequal access to the tactical means of achieving their aims because they live in a patriarchal society within which male power has institutional support. In this way, she shows how class and gender have interacted in complex ways to produce hierarchies of power and prestige in professional work.

Principal Findings

(i) *Power in the professions*

Members of professions often believe that they possess distinctive characteristics which warrant their privileged status in the labour market. However, sociologists argue that it is more useful to see professions, not as special kinds of occupation *per se*, but rather as a mode of controlling occupational activities. Indeed, it is in order to highlight the importance of political processes, such as the ability to define certain occupational tasks as requiring special knowledge and skills, in the definition of some occupations as professions that Witz uses the term 'professional project': professions are the outcome of political struggles and are not pre-given. Historically, the core of the professional project has been the attempt to secure a linkage between *education* and *occupation*.

> Professionalization is thus an attempt to translate one order of scarce resources – special knowledge and skills – into another – social and economic rewards. (Larson, 1977: xvii in Witz, 1992, p.57)

This translation is commonly secured through two different kinds of means: *autonomous* and *heteronomous* means of professionalization. This is a distinction between means which are primarily defined or created by professional groups themselves, which are autonomous means and those which are chiefly secured through other social groups, including the state, which are heteronomous means (see *Figure 8.1*, p.91).

However, while sociologists have been sceptical about professionals' rationalization of their relatively powerful position in the labour market, they have often taken for granted the male domination of professions. Indeed, the successful professional projects of men (such as that of doctors) have tended to be taken as exemplary of the process of professionalization. The result of this is that women's professional projects (that of nurses, for example), because they have generally been unsuccessful, are usually deemed semi-professions or are seen as lesser in some way. Witz asks why this is so. Is it simply an accident that women are not well represented in most professions? Or is it a result of how professions have come to be defined in a gender biased way?

In answering this question, Witz uncovers the struggles between men and women over the ability to create, control access to and promotion within, professions. She documents how the gender of the actors and broader structures of male dominance, organized in the state, universities and training agencies, made a difference to both the form and the outcome of male and female professional projects. She concludes that professions are not immune from the social processes which generate and sustain gender inequality in other areas of employment.

These processes include: (i) *exclusion*, the attempt to exclude women from entry to an occupation; and (ii) *segregation*, the separation of so-called men's jobs from so-called women's jobs and their differential reward by, for example, making use of definitions of skill which favour men at the expense of women. These strategies, identified in historical and contemporary analyses of the labour market by Hartmann (1979), Cockburn (1983), Walby (1986) and others, were used by organized, working class men to delimit and restrict working class women's participation in paid work. Witz shows how middle class men have used these and other strategies in their own attempts to secure the best positions in the labour market. In this way, she demonstrates that the gender of actors was a factor in the creation of professions because men and women had unequal access to the various resources which were necessary to stake a successful claim to 'professional status' in the 19th and early 20th centuries.

(ii) *Historical methods*

Witz seeks to uncover the historical roots of the current gender hierarchy among health care professions, namely, medical men, midwives, nurses and radiographers. To this end, she draws on documentary sources including parliamentary records, government publications, the records of professional bodies, medical journals (for example, *Nursing Record, British Journal of Radiology*), and biographical accounts by key participants. These were collected via a kind of detective work: tracking down references, painstakingly studying archives, coming up against dead-ends, starting again and following up promising leads.

Historical sociology often faces problems stemming from the incompleteness and partiality of historical sources. These sources are primarily documentary (the actors themselves obviously cannot be interviewed), and are thus likely to represent the views of those in positions of power or prestige, those whose decisions, thoughts and point of view were deemed worthy of record, rather than those whose lives were shaped by the decisions of others. To mitigate this difficulty, Witz endeavoured to make use of as wide a range of sources as possible. Once uncovered, documents are studied to reveal the negotiations, disputes and conflicts between different social groups about the boundaries between, and content of, occupations. Witz further ensures that the different kinds of sources are placed in their historical context, and competing accounts are carefully weighed against each other, by locating different versions of events in terms of the interests of the participants and the writers.

(iii) *Whose history is it anyway?*

Witz argues that occupational strategies may be gendered in two senses: first, the participants come into the labour market with identities based in oppositional understandings of gender, and so gender identity may form the basis of political solidarity and division; and second, gendered criteria of exclusion or inclusion may be inbuilt features of occupational strategies. Drawing on her historical data, Witz shows that the case of the project to professionalize medicine was male-biased in both senses: men organized together to exclude women, and made use of gendered criteria of exclusion, including the condition that all those seeking access to the medical register be trained at universities and professional corporations which systematically denied entry to women. But how did this happen?

In 1858, the Medical (Registration) Act gave legal definition to the term 'qualified medical practitioner' by setting up a state-sponsored register of qualified practitioners. It thus provided the basis for a (heteronomous) type of professional control in that it provided the basis for a monopoly of medical skills to be established. In itself, however, this was not a patriarchal form of control. The Act's parliamentary sponsor, William Cowper-Temple, had not intended to exclude women; indeed, 'The Act of 1858 spoke generally of "persons", and did not make any exclusion of female persons as compared with males' (*Hansard*, CCXXXX, 1876). However, gendered exclusionary mechanisms were introduced by university medical faculties, the various Royal Colleges of Physicians and of Surgeons and other medical corporations, as well as teaching hospitals. Men actively organized to exclude women from medical education and examination in all of the institutions which allowed entry onto the medical register.

The reasons for this exclusion were often expressed in moral terms. For example, a memorandum from male medical students about the admission of female students presented to the Middlesex Hospital Medical School Committee stated that, 'the promiscuous assemblage of the sexes in the same class is a dangerous innovation likely to lead to results of an unpleasant character' (*Minutes of the Middlesex Hospital Medical School Committee*, Vol. III, 1861, Appendix I). At other times, no justification apart from custom was deemed necessary. When the Royal College of Surgeons turned down Elizabeth Garrett's request in 1861 to attend lectures on obstetrics with a view to sitting the examination for their diploma in midwifery, the solicitor of the College declared:

> 'that although there was nothing in the Charter relating to the examination for the certificate of qualification in midwifery showing an intention that such certificates should be confined to male persons, yet that on the whole his impression was that there was quite sufficient doubt as to women having any right to claim to be examined to justify the College refusing to depart from the practice which had hitherto prevailed of admitting only men to examination for the certificate of midwifery . . .' (Cope, 1959, p.21)

(iv) *Strategies for professionalization*

Rather than simply documenting these disputes, Witz draws on the concepts of exclusion and segregation to develop an analytical framework to identify common patterns amongst these and other struggles in projects of professionalization. Indeed, she redefines these occupational strategies more precisely as exclusionary, inclusionary, demarcationary and dual closure strategies (see *Figure 8.2*, p.92).

The practices described above are examples of *exclusionary* practices, which Witz defines as involving the downwards exercise of power as

Bibliography and Further Reading

Allen, I. (1988), *Any Room at the Top? A Study of Doctors and Their Careers*, London, Policy Studies Institute.
Bradley, H. (1989), *Men's Work, Women's Work*, Cambridge, Polity Press.
Cockburn, C. (1983), *Brothers: Male Dominance and Technological Change*, London, Pluto Press.
Connell, R. W. (1987), *Gender and Power*, Cambridge, Polity Press.
Crompton, R. and Sanderson, K. (1989), *Gendered Jobs and Social Change*, London, Unwin Hyman.
Hartmann, H. (1979), 'Capitalism, patriarchy and job segregation by sex' in Z. R. Eisenstein (ed.) *Capitalist Patriarchy and the Case for Socialist Feminism*, New York, Monthly Review Press.
Larson, M. (1977), *The Rise of Professionalism*, California, University of California Press.
Turner, B. S. (1987), *Medical Power and Social Knowledge*, London, Sage.
Walby, S. (1986), *Patriarchy at Work*, Cambridge, Polity Press.

Appendices

Autonomous means	*Heteronomous means*
Systematic training and testing	Registration and licensing
Institutionally located in professional schools and the modern university	Institutionally located in the state

Figure 8.1   Modern means of professionalisation

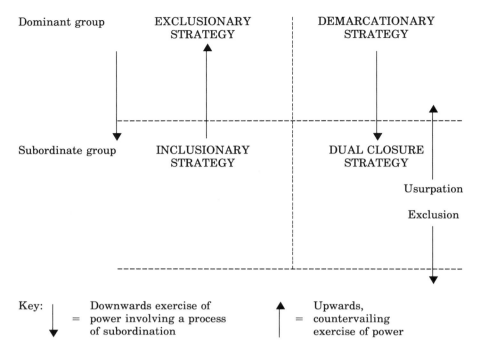

Figure 8.2 Strategies of occupational closure: a conceptual model (ibid., Figure 2.1, p.45)

9

Gender and Inequality in Organizations

Cynthia Cockburn (1991), *In the Way of Women: Men's Resistance to Sex Inequality in Organizations*, Basingstoke, Macmillan.

Lisa Adkins

The 'Backlash' Against Feminism

Cynthia Cockburn's *In the Way of Women* is a study of equal opportunities (EO) policies and practices in organizations. Whilst it pays attention to a variety of equality measures, including action on race, disability and homosexuality, it is primarily concerned with women's struggles for equality. More specifically, it focusses on *men's responses* to women's initiatives. This focus is one shared by other recent writing by feminists concerned with negative reactions to the women's liberation movement – a phenomenon commonly referred to as a 'backlash'.

These negative responses have involved a wide ranging set of social practices, including: negative stereotyping of feminists; claims that feminism is redundant and that we are now living in a post-feminist age; and increasing violence towards women. Cockburn argues all these diverse practices are attempts to (re)assert control over women in reaction to the articulation of feminist demands and that systematic analysis of this phenomenon is long overdue. Her special focus on *organizations* is unusual because much of the discussion around the 'backlash' to date has focussed on negative *cultural* responses to feminism, for instance on oppressive representations of feminists in the media (Faludi, 1991; French, 1992).

Why Organizations?

Like other materialist feminists, Cockburn allocates special significance to organizations in the construction of power relations between men and women. She sees them as 'precisely and uniquely the means

by which power is effected' (Cockburn, 1991, p.17). As principal
purveyors of power, organizations are key to the construction and
reproduction of male dominated social relations. They are the pillars
of patriarchy, the places where power relations between men and
women are made and maintained. They are therefore central to the
making and *unmaking* of gender, i.e. they are primary sites of feminist
struggle.

Cockburn points out there has been a certain amount of ambiguity
among feminists as to how this struggle in organizations should best
be carried out. Many have been sceptical about attempts to bring
about change from insider positions, fearing feminism would become
co-opted. Nonetheless, increasingly feminists *have* moved into institutions (as a result of previous rounds of feminist struggle) and *have*
attempted to deploy feminist strategies for change within organizational settings. How has this worked out? Cockburn examines the
responses of individual men and male dominated organizations to one
particularly common form of feminist strategies in organizations:
those which go under the banner of 'equality of opportunity'. By this
she means both women's own demands for workplace equality, including the right to paid work, to occupations with fair pay, training and
prospects; and policies introduced into organizations on behalf of
women by managers and owners.

The Study

Cockburn carried out a comparative study of four large organizations
based in the UK. These were a large private sector retail firm, a government department, a local council, and a national trade union. The
common feature of these organizations was that each had a formal,
publicly stated commitment to equality of opportunity and each had
an 'equality infrastructure' – which included committees and equality
personnel such as officers and advisers. In other respects they were, of
course, very different.

- 'High Street Retail' was a large business with a chain of shops
  employing nearly 30,000 people, three quarters of whom were
  women, typically employed in manual and routine non-manual jobs.
  Cockburn describes this company as a typical capitalist enterprise:
  its aim was profit maximization, it had an authoritian management
  style and weak trade union organization. At the time of the
  research, some of the old rigidities of the firm were, however, being
  rocked by measures introduced in the face of a crisis of profitability.
  These included the introduction of more innovative, risk taking
  managers; new drives towards publicity and image; and a greater
  orientation towards customer service.

- The government department, 'The Service', was a conventional
  state bureaucratic organization. It had a formal, hierarchical structure, a strong white collar, 'pen-pushing' culture, and was heavily

influenced by past conventions regarding rules and procedures. It had tens of thousands of employees located in a head office and in divisional and district offices up and down the country – most of whom (90%) were in clerical/administrative jobs and 65% of whom were women located in the lower to middle grades. The upper grades of clerks, however, tended mostly to be men. 'The Service' was run by an elite group of workers who were mostly white middle class (Oxbridge) men.

Despite its traditionalism, 'The Service' too was experiencing some change. In particular it was losing some of its old formality. An old system of class privilege was being replaced by a meritocratic one and a labour shortage had meant that many entry requirements had been relaxed.

- The 'Local Authority' was run by an elected local body and was responsible for delivering services such as schools and housing. This organization (like other local authorities) relied heavily on manual labour in the provision of these services and many of the manual workers (especially the lower graded ones) were women. This organization was particularly interesting from Cockburn's point of view because it had previously pursued a variety of innovatory strategies against various forms of discrimination. These had gained it a considerable reputation. This organization provided Cockburn with 'a base line for thoroughgoing efforts on the equality front' (ibid., p.3).

- Her final organization, the 'Trade Union', was also run by an elected body. This membership organization supported mostly low paid manual workers in the public sector. It had two thirds of a million members; three quarters of whom were women. Three quarters of these women worked part-time. On average the women members' hourly pay was 80% of their male counterparts. The union was structured and operated through elected local branches, regional and national committees and councils. Despite women constituting by far the majority of the membership, every level of the union structure was male dominated. From shop steward to national committee level, men characteristically filled and controlled its posts and positions.

Cockburn's choice of these different organizations meant she could assess in what ways different organizational features, such as an overarching commitment to profit maximization, or a formal bureaucratic structure or being a representative body, related to the development of forms of equality of opportunity strategy. She could therefore ask 'are there particular features of organizations which pull against or contradict such strategies? or are there some which are more conducive to equality, allowing space for equality of opportunity measures to be pursued?'

Research Design

To make such assessments and address her overall research questions, Cockburn used a variety of qualitative research techniques: observation, documentary investigation and the extensive use of in-depth interviews (she carried out over 200), supplemented by informal conversations and small group discussions. All the interviews were taped and the majority fully transcribed. Given the nature of Cockburn's research questions, and in particular the phenomena she wished to expose, the use of qualitative techniques was clearly appropriate. She needed to be able to see and analyse social relationships, processes and contradictions; to understand each organization, the way it worked (both formally and informally), the way its equality measures were developed, the exact content of these measures, how they were implemented, who opposed and/or who supported them and why. These could only be discovered by in-depth, detailed research.

The research took two years to complete. Approximately two months were spent in each organization, interviewing, observing and reading documents. The majority of the interviewees were selected on two principles. First, key personnel involved with equal opportunity policy were chosen. This necessarily included some, and in some cases most, of the top management, senior personnel management and specialist equality staff (such as women's officers and race equality officers). Second, a sample of employees/members 'down the line' were interviewed. To obtain such a sample, random selections were made from employee lists which were stratified by grade.

Because the study was mainly about men's responses to equality the overall sample was mostly male, but approximately one third of it was female, as Cockburn wanted to obtain women's views of each organization, its equality policies and men's reactions.

In addition to these interviews, for each case study Cockburn also interviewed women and men who were willing to be identified as lesbian or gay, and women and men with disabilities. She also made sure that around 15% of all those interviewed were black. This meant that the views of groups often excluded from sociological research were represented.

The interview questions were mainly about feelings and reactions to EO, and, once transcribed, the interview data was sorted thematically for analysis.

Principal Findings

In the presentation of her research findings, Cockburn provides a rich blend of description and analysis, highlighting particular themes as she goes. Her most significant finding was that all manner of impediments operated to prevent the achievement of equality in all four organizations. These had kept EO to a limited, minimum, fairly ineffective agenda. She divides these impediments into two interacting types: institutional – which 'include structures, procedures and rules' (ibid., p.45) which stall women's advancement in organizations; and cultural impediments which arise in everyday 'discourse and interaction' (ibid., p.45). Various forms of both of these impediments operated in all the organizations. Here there is space to give just a few examples.

(i) *Institutional impediments*

At High Street Retail, for instance, some of the major impediments to equality of opportunity were institutional. Specifically, the lesser value attached to women's labour compared to men's in this organization was incorporated into the main aim of the organization – profit maximization. The organization directly benefited from the relative undervaluing of women's labour: it kept its labour costs low. Cockburn shows how this incorporation of gender inequality into the structure of High Street Retail was one of the main reasons why the equality of opportunity measures introduced into the organization were weak and failed to have any systematic impact. Despite being a trend setter in the area of equality of opportunity in the private sector, all the equality measures at High Street Retail only improved the position of a small number of (relatively senior) women. The majority (of low paid and low status women workers) remained untouched. To have equality of opportunity which dealt with women *inclusively* (from low paid, part time shop workers to senior managers), which is what equality activists in the organization had argued for, would have involved a series of measures (including job-revaluations, regradings, and narrowing wage differentials), which would have flown in the face of the aims of the organization: i.e. accumulation and profit. In other words, the organization was willing to concede some equality measures to a very small number of women in relatively senior positions; but not to women as a whole – for to do so would be far too costly.

But even the 'gains' made for women in more senior positions had their down side. For although more women had got into management recently, particularly store management, because of the changes in the company, High Street Retail was simultaneously attaching less significance to this job than it had in the past. Its focus had moved to marketing, advertising and public relations. Indeed, some personnel managers saw the entry of women into store management very instrumentally. Women constituted the optimal labour force for this job as they had a 'nice way' with customers. This example shows once again how gender inequality is built into capitalist relations. The movement of women into store management had less to do with equality of opportunity than to do with this particular company's latest move to increase profitability – improving customer service.

The downgrading of jobs as women enter into them was also found

in one of Cockburn's other organizations – the government department, The Service, where the pre-eminent equality issue for women
was obtaining equal chances of promotion. There was very little
external recruitment in The Service and it was, therefore, primarily
through promotion that women could reach higher grades. Previously, promotion had been governed strictly by time served, which
disadvantaged women because of their often broken careers. Moreover, promotion had been controlled by white men who 'had simply
been reproducing themselves' (ibid., p.54), i.e. they promoted other
white men.

This institutional impediment to women's advancement was
removed through EO measures which amended the time honoured
rule and also made the promotion process more accountable, in the
hopes of preventing the marking-down of women and ethnic minorities. These EO measures, together with the more general relaxation
of some of the rules and procedures at The Service did produce some
change in the organization. Already dominant in the clerical grades,
women began to move into the higher, professional jobs within them,
and the number of ethnic minorities in these grades also began to
increase, albeit in the lower and middle ranking jobs.

But again, this cannot be read as a straightforward case of the
opening up of jobs and a democratization of the organization. Over the
years women's ceiling had shifted upwards from upper clerical, to
junior professional, and it was currently at the step between junior
and middle professional grades, but they still had great difficulty
moving into the middle and higher professional grades where they
continued to be seen as anomalies: 'it was still the bowler hat brigade
they were looking for' (ibid., p.56). Moreover, although women were
now getting into the junior professional grades these jobs were again
simultaneously being downgraded. They no longer had the status
they had had when women were excluded from them. As women
began to move into the junior level professional grades, men no longer
found these jobs attractive. They treated them not as 'serious' career
occupations, as they had done previously, but in an instrumental
manner – as simply a means to an ends, most commonly as a way of
receiving training in order to get 'proper' jobs in the private sector.

(ii) *Cultural impediments*

Cockburn also reveals another very important aspect of men's
responses to the movement of women into jobs from which they had
previously been excluded – the creation of a culture of resistance. Men
actively engaged in specifically oppositional activities which made it
very difficult for women to do well and which acted as a means of
control of women. This culture of resistance was particularly evident
in The Service's clerical grades, which had seen the greatest influx of
women, and where men felt hard-done by and resentful towards
women. This resentment surfaced in a number of different ways,

including the unwillingness of subordinate men to accept the authority of women and outright hostility towards successful women. As one man said, 'I haven't got to work for this *little girl*, have I?' (ibid., p.67). Senior women were constructed as undeserving – as having cheated on the promotion rules and using the equality measures to gain promotion rather than possessing the required competences and skills. In addition, men also constructed women in power as being masculine – as not 'proper' women. This culture of resistance not only made the day-to-day life of women in power in the organization very difficult – it also acted as a deterrent to women attempting to compete with men for promotion and authority. To do so would mean becoming the object of resentment and ridicule. Moreover it was a successful strategy, for its operation meant that women were not applying for professional training. One woman did not do so because she feared 'I might lose my friends' (ibid., p.69).

One of the themes Cockburn pulls out of the Trade Union case study is that resistance to equality measures came not simply from the archetypal macho union hero, but also from, younger, 'new' men. Indeed such men were identified by women in all four of the organizations. Unlike the 'old guard', these men said they accepted the presence of women in organizations, but they nevertheless, operated a highly sexualized discourse directed at women which placed them in a double bind. If they ignored or attempted to resist the men's chatting ups or sexual innuendos, they were marginalized or labelled as spoilsports. But if they joined in they were in danger of getting their fingers burnt by, for instance, being labelled obscene. Thus, when a woman at The Service responded to the office culture by sending sexy birthday cards to colleagues, her male senior manager found her shocking: 'She sends people cards that I think, God! Oh dear!' (ibid., p.156). The operation of this kind of sexualized discourse across all four of the organization was a constant source of inequality between men and women – serving to produce and reproduce power relations and therefore acting as an impediment to equality. But EO policies had little impact in the area of sexuality. Indeed this was an area which was often downplayed by those specialists involved. At High Street Retail for instance, the equality manager, feeling it was an explosive issue, downplayed the issue of sexual harassment, fearing that raising it would damage the rest of the equality strategy.

Cockburn did find some variations in the EO activities in the four organizations, in particular she found that in the representative organizations (the Trade Union and the Local Authority), where there was a recognition that to some extent or another they should be democratic, there was more space available to explore and experiment with feminist ideas and practice. But despite this variation, overall, on the basis of her evidence, Cockburn concludes that in *all* the organizations EO has been a disappointment, primarily because the agenda was so restricted.

She suggests that there are two main ways in which EO is kept to a minimum in organizations. First, organizations tend to use limited methods to pursue 'equality' – choosing, for instance, high profile, cost-free measures (which can be of advantage to the organization), rather then more expensive, more effective ones. Second, there is the problem of men whose active resistance to equality measures also keeps EO to a limited, restricted agenda. By far the majority of men she encountered in the organizations were, in Cockburn's words, 'engaged in a damage limitation exercise', attempting to (and indeed succeeding in) keeping equality of opportunity to a minimum. Even the few men who were supportive of, and sometimes active around, equality issues, tended to have a shorter agenda than women. In particular they rejected any explicitly feminist ideas and practices.

Critical Observations

Cockburn's study offers us a compelling mix of original empirical research, analysis, and practical recommendations. It undoubtedly furthers our understandings of the ways in which power relations between men and women in organizations are currently constructed, articulated and constituted. To date, sociologists who have engaged with it have found much to praise and relatively little to criticize, and many of her findings and parts of her analysis are already being incorporated unproblematically into a (new and expanding) literature which seeks to unravel the relationship between gender divisions and organizational hierarchies (see, for example, chapters in Savage and Witz, 1992).

Jeff Hearn and Wendy Parkin (1992) have, however, argued that although it is packed full of new, exciting, empirical material, there is a general absence of theoretical development. They suggest, for instance, that Cockburn's study provides material which can be used to enhance our understandings of social divisions, the relationships between different oppressions, and even to refine our understandings of concepts such as patriarchy and capitalism. But, rather disappointingly, the author herself does not pursue these issues in any sustained manner. Nor does Cockburn really pursue the theoretical implications of her evidence in terms of organization theory. She certainly says that her findings suggest the need for a reconceptualization of organizational power – particularly of the way in which it is gendered – but she does not suggest how.

A further problem with the study is the difficulty of telling if the impediments to equality recorded by Cockburn represent a new phenomenon (namely a blacklash to the articulation of feminist demands), or if they are part and parcel of forms of the subordination of women which have long been present in organizations. She provides plenty of evidence to suggest that there are pervasive negative responses to equality strategies; but she does not demonstrate that these responses are specifically different from processes of control of women which pre-existed the women's liberation movement or which characterize organizations without EO policies and practices. Of course, both operate at the same time, but it is important to be able to make the distinction. To know whether we are living in a period of backlash requires demonstrating how backlash differs from other modes of control.

One way of attempting to identify a specific backlash would have been to include one organization in the study where there were no strategies for equality of opportunity in operation – one where there had been no equality activism or pressure placed on the organization to adopt equality measures. The inclusion of such a case would have made it possible to compare forms of control of women operating in the different organizational settings, and to distinguish those which they share in common from those where demands for equality operate.

Cockburn in fact provides us with very little indication of how she came to choose the four organizations – apart from the fact that they all had a formal commitment to EO. Indeed, there is very little discussion of methodology throughout, and although few would question that qualitative techniques were the most appropriate for this kind of study, there are problems with these methods to which she does not draw our attention. For instance, it is difficult to make general claims from in-depth research into particular cases; and studies of particular cases at particular points in time (or 'snap-shots') can actually be misrepresentative. Particular current or recent phenomena are noted, but other (perhaps more important) occasional or long term ones can be completely missed. This is certainly a problem which applies when relatively short periods of time (two months) are spent investigating each of the cases.

Studies carried out over short periods of time also present problems in terms of the reliability of the evidence. In Cockburn's case, although she used a variety of methods, she actually relies much more on interviews than anything else to find out about responses to EO. But how do we know that the material she gained in the interviews represented the resistance operating in each of the organizations? Some of the forms of resistance were gleaned from different interviewee accounts of a particular event or occurrence, but on the whole such corroboration could not take place, and it was not possible to compare different sources and sorts of evidence because of the 'in and out' style of the study. An extended period of fieldwork in just one organization on the other hand – involving repeat interviews, more 'hanging around' and more systematic observation – might have thrown up other forms of resistance and enabled the researcher to make a more reliable assessment of the general level of resistance. Cockburn gained a great deal by comparing four organizations, especially since she found common reactions to EO, but, on the other hand, it has to be asked what was lost by not being immersed in any particular one.

Bibliography and Further Reading

Cockburn, C. (1991), *In the Way of Women: Men's Resistance to Sex Equality in Organizations*, Basingstoke, Macmillan.

Dworkin, A. (1983), *Right Wing Women*, London, The Women's Press.

Faludi, S. (1991), *Backlash – The Undeclared War Against Women*, London, Chatto and Windus.

French, M. (1992), *The War Against Women*, London, Hamish Hamilton.

Hearn, J. and Parkin, W. (1987), *'Sex' at 'Work': The Power and Paradox of Organization Sexuality*, Brighton, Wheatsheaf.

Hearn, J. and Parkin, W. (1992), Review of 'In the Way of Women', in *Sociology*,
Vol. 26, No. 3, 1992, pp.515–517.

Kramerae, C. and Spender, D. (eds.), (1992), *The Knowledge Explosion*, New York, Pergamon.

Leidholdt, D. and Raymond, J. (eds.), (1990), *The Sexual Liberals and the Attack on Feminism*, New York, Pergamon.

O'Reilly, E. (1992), *Masterminds of the Right*, Dublin, Attic Press.

Savage, M. and Witz, A. (eds.), (1992), *Gender and Bureaucracy*, Oxford, Blackwell.

Appendices

9.1 *Male union employees talking about their views on the equality measures.*

(Cockburn, 1991, p.118 and p.124):

'I see it creeping in. I see it creeping in . . . [said . . . bitterly]. People voted for the best person, the one who was going to be able to do a better job. But now I've a sneaky feeling we're getting away from that. Whereby a woman is getting voted on just because she's a woman. But who's going to do the best job? That doesn't come into it. "We want a woman". And in many cases the candidate is being pressurized to put herself forward. "Go on, you have a go at it." I think it's bad for the Union. It's bad for the Union.'

'As a man you can sometimes feel a bit threatened by it all. For instance I'm not sure if I'd happily step aside in my job and allow a woman to come into it. Or if I had the opportunity of becoming, say, general secretary that I would *not* do it because I thought a woman ought to come through.'

9.2 *Young woman (junior office worker) reporting on sexualization at work* (ibid., p.139):

'I get remarks all the time . . . Most men comment on my boobs. They say things about them to each other. I walk past and they're just like *that* [She mimicked someone staring at her chest.] This man [she named a senior person], I was talking to him and he was just standing staring at me. He didn't even look at my face, he was like *this* the whole time . . . I get comments all the time. This man [she named a different manager] . . . he makes so many comments, like, "Every time you walk in the room we all swoon at you." And whenever I go into the filing room he'll squeeze in there and pretend to try to get something out of a file. And he'll say things. One time I had a T-shirt with some writing [she indicated her chest.] And one of them peered and said "What's that?" Then all of a sudden I had about six men all over me, all staring, saying "Oh what's that, what's that." It's every minute . . . If I wear a skirt I get comments about my legs or something. I just dress scruffy, I dress in black so that they won't say anything.'

9.3 *Men's comments on senior women at The Service* (ibid., pp.67/69):

. . . 'hard as nails
. . . tough as old boots
. . . get a bit emotional
. . . find it difficult to be ruthless
. . . lack a bit of judgement
. . . bossy, pushy, absolute bastards
. . . ferocious . . . get a kick out of lording it over men'

10

Women's Work in Farming Families

Sarah Whatmore (1991), *Farming Women: gender, work and family enterprise*, Basingstoke, Macmillan.

Anne Witz

Farming Women

Whatmore's empirical study of farming wives aims to make visible their contribution to the family farm. She shows how farming women are almost exclusively responsible for domestic household labour, but how they also engage in agricultural and non-agricultural farm labour and sometimes in paid work off the farm. She examines similarities and differences in the work and experiences of farming wives on three types of farm: family farms, 'transitional' farms and business farms. She also looks at the extent to which women own and control land and capital on farms. Whatmore's study demonstrates how the division of labour in family farming is structured by patriarchy, particularly in the sense that it is women's status as 'wives' which is central in shaping their obligations to assume the main responsibility for household work and to engage in farm work. It also indicates how ownership and control of land and capital is structured by patrilineage, which places economic power in the hands of male members of the household.

Research Design

Whatmore employed two complementary levels of data collection and analysis: an *extensive* level, using a questionnaire survey method to describe the pattern of familial gender relations on farms; and an *intensive* level, using ethnographic methods and consisting of a small number of case studies designed to provide an interpretive framework for understanding farming wives' own experiences and gender relations in farming families.

The research was carried out in two rural areas in southern England, one in west Dorset, the other in the Metropolitan Green Belt (MGB) around London. These two areas were selected because they represented different kinds of farming systems and rural environments. Background information and a base-line sample of 86 farms in the MGB and 99 farms in west Dorset had already been gathered from a wider research project.

The survey of farming women was conducted through a postal questionnaire administered to a sample of 135 women. The questionnaire was accompanied by an introductory letter and a stamped addressed envelope, followed by one reminder letter. The response rate was 60%. Information was collected on: the women's social background and current household structure; their work activities including housework, agricultural work, non-agricultural work (such as bookkeeping) and paid work off the farm (such as teaching); their legal and financial stakes in the farm; their involvement in decision-making and management; and their community activities (see *Passage 10.1*, p.114). The final question in the postal survey asked women if they would be willing to be involved in the second stage of the research. Six women were selected to be the subjects of the intensive research.

This stage involved a more qualitative method. It combined a case study method of analysis with a less formalized method of data collection, described by Whatmore as 'cumulative interviewing'. This combination of case study and informal interviews, referred to as 'taped conversations', represented an attempt to adapt some of the ethnographic techniques associated with participant observation to a research situation where participant observation was inappropriate (because of the geographically dispersed nature of the research subjects). The case study exercise consisted of a quarterly visit to each farm during which time the woman was asked about her work and position on the farm. There were three key characteristics of the 'cumulative interviewing' method:

First, a relationship of trust and familiarity with the farming wives was built up over a period of time, in this case one year. Initially a semi-structured interview format was used but later informal conversations between the researcher and the farming wives became more common. In this way, the interview process is culmulative, as each visit builds upon the knowledge, interest and trust developed during the previous visit.

Second, the objective was to get beyond the limitations of a taped interview, where the tape is turned off once enough information has been extracted from the research subject. Instead, visits lasted half a day or a day, so conversation and activity preceded and followed the turning on and off of the tape-recorder and Whatmore actually got involved in what the women were doing.

Third, by extending visits beyond the time it took to interview women, it was also possible to meet with, observe and listen to other members of the family within a group setting, getting more of a feel for farming family life.

The data collected consisted of six hours of taped conversation for each researth subject, as well as field notes and other contextual material. Rather than asking farming wives to keep a written time-budget diary, Whatmore incorporated a 'time-diary' exercise into the recorded conversations, asking women to describe their activities on the day previous to the visit.

The survey data enabled Whatmore to analyse the aggregate pattern of familial gender divisions in the farm labour process, whilst the case study data enabled her to reconstruct a picture of the everyday experiences of farming wives, in which their individuality is retained and their own voices allowed to speak.

Principal Findings

The study concentrated on three main areas: the gender division of labour on farms; women's everyday experiences as farm wives; and the ways in which small-scale production for the market is based on the labour of the family (i.e. how what Marxists refer to as 'petty commodity production' involves a familial and gendered division of labour).

(i) Women's work and property

Using women's answers to the questionnaire survey, Whatmore describes the familial gender division of labour on farms. Farm wives' involvement in domestic household labour, agricultural and non-agricultural labour, and off-farm labour is explored. Domestic household labour is allocated almost exclusively to women, but there is no straightforward link between the extent of farm wives' domestic responsibilities and the extent of their participation in other forms of labour. In particular, farm wives' participation in non-domestic labour was found by Whatmore to be unrelated to their stage in the family life-cycle such as, for example, how many children they had or how old they were.

Domestic household labour is the main area of responsibility and labour activity of the farm wife. Women also play a key administrative role on the farm, engaging on a regular basis in various forms of non-agricultural farm labour such as book-keeping, dealing with enquiries, and running errands for the business (see *Table 10.1*, p.113). In addition, women showed high levels of participation in livestock feeding/rearing and manual agricultural labour, although this is generally restricted to seasonal activities like haymaking. Farming wives also engage in *commoditized* forms of domestic household labour; that is to say women sell for money food and consumption goods normally produced for their own families. In Dorset, this is most likely to be offering bed and breakfast to tourists, whilst in MGB selling fresh

farm produce from farm shops was more common. Few farming wives
are employed off the farm.

(ii) *Wives in the farm labour process*

Wives' work was found by Whatmore to have three main characteristics. First, wives were primarily responsible for domestic household
labour. Second, their work was largely responsive to others' needs,
rather than initiatory and self-determined. Thirdly, it was characterized by the simultaneous performance of several tasks associated with
farming women's multiple roles as wives, mothers and reserve farm
labour.

Whatmore draws on her qualitative research data to convey the
everyday experiences of farming wives. Consider, for example,
Hannah Green's description of her day, which illustrates how farming
wives engage simultaneously in a diverse range of labour tasks (see
Passage 10.2, p.116).

All the women disliked domestic household tasks, particularly
housework and doing the laundry, but accepted that these tasks were
their responsibility, as the following two extracts demonstrate:

> 'I hate the housework and always have. I have to do that myself as no
> one else does it. I think perhaps that's why I've got so many jobs [in the
> farm business] because I don't like doing that . . . I only do them because
> no one else does and then the whole thing falls down.' (Gayle Brown)
> (Whatmore, 1991)

> 'There's a conflict of roles all round . . . because the cows I'm supposed
> to be in charge of and as I say I should be out there every day looking
> at them and checking them but I'm not because I'm doing other things.
> I'm either doing the flowers [she has a dried-flower business] or, like this
> morning, I just did housework which is very boring, I really do hate that,
> but one has to do it.' (Julie Church) (ibid.)

Whatmore analyses how ideologies of wifehood inform the roles
assigned to women and the ways in which women make sense of their
experiences as farming wives. Women's status and identity as 'wives'
is constructed in one of two ways, as 'farming women' or as 'incorporated wives'. 'Farming women' describes the role and status of wives
on the family labour farm, where they have a distinctive status which
extends beyond the domestic household into extensive involvement in
agricultural tasks. 'Farming women's' contributions, whether domestic or agricultural, to the family farm are highly valued and regarded
as an integral part of the collective family entreprise. On the family
labour farm the kitchen/parlour is at the centre of life on the farms,
not just for farming women but for all members of the family. By contrast, the 'incorporated wife' is found on the 'family business farm',
where agricultural work is more extensively commoditized, and they

conform more closely to the middle class 'housewife' model. The 'domestic' domain is more clearly segregated from the 'working farm' and there is a more rigid division of labour between domestic and farm tasks. When 'incorporated wives' engage in non-domestic, farming tasks this is usually on terms set by their husbands, who tend actively to control the farming business and dictate the terms of women's involvement. Compared to 'farming women', 'incorporated wives' tended to express greater dissatisfaction with the gendered division of labour on farms.

Whatmore argues that these different experiences of 'farming women' and 'incorporated wives' indicate an important shift in women's experiences of farming life. 'Farming women' have a central position in a household production system centred on family labour and organized around the conjugal household. 'Incorporated farm wives' have a marginal position in a household production system based on family capital and organized around patrilineal kinship relations, where fathers and sons play a more dominant role in farm business. Given the gradual demise of family labour farms and the increase in family business farms, we are seeing a shift in the role of farming wives (as 'farming women' become less common and 'incorporated wives' more so) and, thus, in the gender division of labour in farming families.

(iii) *Commodification and the family farm*

Whatmore's study of different types of family farming enterprises aims to demonstrate how gender relations and the subordination of women as 'wives' are central to an understanding of the nature of labour relations in family farming. She uses case studies of six family farms to show how kinship, household and enterprise intersect in different ways at different levels of commoditization and in different local contexts. Commoditization describes 'the process by which the family household and farm enterprise are tied into the wider market economy in such a way that their form and conditions of existence are increasingly structured by it' (Whatmore, 1991, p.7). Whatmore uses the term 'domestic political economy' to capture the interdependence of family and enterprise on farms.

Overall, Whatmore suggests that women occupy key positions in farms with a low level of commoditization and where family *labour* is crucial in the workings of the farm, but that they become more marginalized in business farms where the regime is centred on family *property*. Contrast for example, the family-centred labour process at Holly Farm (see *Figure 10.1*, p.114) with the more complex labour process at Naylors Farm, which involves a mix of domestic, agricultural, non-agricultural and off-farm labour as well as much more hired wage labour (see *Figure 10.2*, p.114).

On Holly Farm, Mr and Mrs Green, their younger daughter and her husband (who live a quarter of a mile away in the village) make up the family labour team. The farm labour process at Holly Farm operates entirely on family labour, employing only one additional hired worker at haymaking and contract labour for hay baling. The main agricultural enterprises are dairying, with a herd of 15 Jersey cows, a beef sideline and a flock of 50 ewes producing lambs for meat. Chickens, turkeys and eggs are also produced on a small scale, principally for household consumption, and two house cows provide milk for the family. Associated with these livestock enterprises are hay and silage activities, and potatoes are grown as a market crop. There is a familial division of labour where Mrs Green does domestic household tasks and agricultural tasks (bringing cows to the milking parlour, cleaning out cow sheds, dealing with poultry and eggs for family consumption and for sale), whilst Mr Green does solely agricultural work. The daughter does a range of agricultural tasks, including the afternoon milking and helping her father in the husbandry operations in the fields. There is a single pool of money, a farm account which is Mr Green's account. However, money income is relatively insignificant to household consumption because, due to Mrs Green's labour, the household is self-sufficient.

Compare Holly Farm to Naylors Farm (which is one of nine farms owned by the Church family). The household at Naylors Farm comprise Mr and Mrs Church and their two teenage children. Both agricultural production and household consumption are extensively tied into the wider market economy, the holding is almost entirely arable and there are an increasing number of non-agricultural enterprises such as a garage and a calor gas business, herb growing, the bulk manufacture of mint and horse-radish sauces (run by Mr Church), as well as flower growing for dried-flower production (run by Mrs Church). Mr Church works full-time on the farm at agricultural and herb enterprises, and his role is largely managerial. There are 14 hired full-time workers, three part-timers and about 20 casual/seasonal workers. Mrs Church has virtually nothing to do with the agricultural work, and her primary role is in the domestic sphere (there is a daily cleaning woman who does the heavy housework). Her other labour tasks include running the dried-flower business (which she set up), the administrative work associated with the cattle breeding enterprise, and keeping the books for her father's cattle business elsewhere. The income from Mrs Church's dried-flower business pays for school fees and family holidays, so is integrated into the household. Otherwise, she receives a housekeeping allowance from Mr Church.

These two case studies reveal the quite different labour processes that characterize family farms and business farms, and demonstrate how, although each have quite marked gendered divisions of labour, nonetheless women's participation in domestic, agricultural, and non-agricultural tasks varies considerably depending on the degree of commoditization of farms. They provide concrete illustrations of Whatmore's distinction between 'farming women' (Mrs Green at Holly Farm) and 'incorporated wives' (Mrs Church at Naylors Farm).

Critical Observations and Conclusion

Questions remain, as Whatmore herself admits, as to whether it is possible to extrapolate key arguments from this study of the gendered structure of family farming to other forms of family-based production in other sectors of the economy. In addition, because Whatmore's main focus is on gender as a structuring principle, there remain issues relating to the significance of generational and age divisions in the organization of family farms. Her study provides data concerning the tasks which women perform, but not about the time they spend performing these tasks. This means that it is not possible to make comparisons between farming women and other women, by looking at the extent of their responsibility for household tasks and the time they spend doing housework.

Sociologists have generally tended to analyse small businesses within the framework of class analysis, as a way of focussing on the fate of the 'petite bourgeoisie' (for example, Bechhofer and Elliot, 1981). Whatmore's study of farming families raises some important, new issues concerning the 'invisible' role of women as wives in small business enterprises. It indicates that sociologists need to study the labour and property relations in small family businesses in the context of shifting gender relations, and not simply in relation to shifting class relations. What tasks do wives perform in family businesses? To what extent are these tasks performed on the basis of their status as wives? Are these tasks valued and rewarded appropriately? What property rights do wives have in family businesses? Are women particularly vulnerable if marriages break up?

The study of small businesses and their reliance on family labour, including the labour of wives, also raises the important question of the intersection between relations of class, gender and race. Some recent research has provided insights into minority women's roles in family businesses, focussing on gender in the context of the ethnic economy (Westwood and Bhachu, 1988). Minority women working with their husbands in small businesses, where they do not receive wages, may be seen to be in a position of dependency as patriarchal relations are reinforced in a manner similar to that described by Whatmore. At the same time, minority women's own consciousness of their position may be to view themselves not as exploited workers, but as committed to a joint stake in the family business. For example, Bhachu's (1988) study of Sikh women revealed how they felt empowered by their involvement in family firms in which they have specific roles and responsibilities, with both access to and control over the products of their labour. Similarly, Baxter and Raw's (1988) analysis of the changing role of Chinese women in family-run food outlets shows how they were initially incorporated as subordinated workers but later become joint participants in family ventures. Like Whatmore's study, these studies of minority women's participation in family businesses demonstrate how it is important not to operate with a view of patriarchal gender relations as unchanging, but to see them as subject to variation, within which women may experience greater or lesser dependence/independence.

Finally, it is useful to draw parallels between Whatmore's study of farming women in Britain and Delphy's (1984) earlier analysis of farming families in France. Delphy also noted how wives on French family farms not only produced food and consumption goods for the family, but also extended these activities to a commercial market where such goods acquire an exchange value. Both studies use a concept of patriarchy to analyse the labour and property relations in farming families. Delphy used her analysis of gender relations in French farming families to develop a general theory of the persistence of a patriarchal (domestic) mode of production alongside a capitalist (industrial) mode of production. She argued that within the patriarchal mode of production husbands are the exploiting class, expropriating the unpaid labour of their wives, who are the exploited class. Whatmore does not agree with Delphy that patriarchy is a separate mode of production from capitalism, but instead integrates her analysis of patriarchy within a Marxist analysis of farming families. Consequently, her analytical framework has more in common with 'dual systems theorists' (like Hartmann and Walby) who believe in the need to examine how capitalism is built on top of patriarchy, so that gender and class relations intersect with one another. Whatmore's study of farming women provides a valuable addition to 'dual systems analyses', enlarging our understanding of how capitalism builds upon and transforms patterns of patriarchal gender relations in modern society.

Bibliography and Further Reading

Baxter, S. and Raw, G. (1988), 'Fast food, fettered work: Chinese women in the ethnic catering industry' in Westwood, S. and Bhachu, P. (eds.).

Bhachu, P. (1988), 'Home and work: Sikh women in Britain' in Westwood, S. and Bhachu, P. (eds.).

Bechhofer, F. and Elliott, B. (eds.) (1981), *The Petite Bourgeoisie*, London, Macmillan.

Delphy, C. (1984), 'The main enemy' in *Close to Home*, London, Hutchinson.

Morris, L. (1990), *The Workings of the Household*, Cambridge, Polity.

Westwood, S. and Bhachu, P. (eds.) (1988), *Enterprising Women: ethnicity, economy and gender relations*, London, Routledge.

Appendices

Table 10.1 Women's agricultural labour (% women on all farms)

	None	Emergency only	Occasional	Regular	All
Book-keeping	26 (33%)	5 (6%)	14 (17%)	34 (42%)	53 (65%)*
Enquiries	0 (—)	0 (—)	19 (24%)	61 (75%)	80 (99%)*
Errands	12 (15%)	4 (5%)	38 (47%)	26 (32%)	68 (84%)*
Manual work	23 (28%)	14 (17%)	17 (21%)	26 (32%)	57 (70%)*
Harvest/haymaking	24 (30%)	19 (24%)	15 (19%)	20 (25%)	54 (68%)*

'All' refers to the proportion of wives participating in some form in each work category
* The rows do not always add up to 100%, owing to non-response
(Whatmore, 1991)

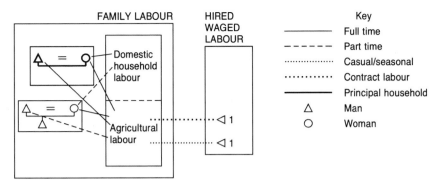

Figure 10.1 The labour process at Holly Farm (ibid., Figure 7.2)

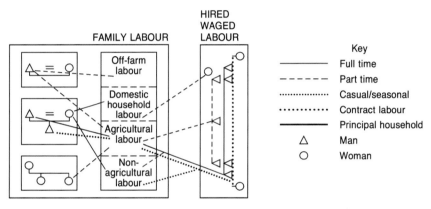

Figure 10.2 The labour process at Naylors Farm (ibid., Figure 7.5)

Passage 10.1: Part of the postal questionnaire concerning work tasks

SECTION B Your Working Day

15. How long is your active/working day (from when you get up to when you go to sleep) in hours?
    (a) on weekdays:
    (b) at weekends:
    (if different from (a))

16. Would you say that you spend most of your active day on activities (tick as appropriate)

	weekday	weekends
(a) in the house?		
(b) on the farm?		
(c) off the farm?		

17. On the domestic front, which of the following activities do you do?

	YES	NO
(a) childcare (including taking children to and from school)		
(b) preparing family meals		
(c) housework		
(d) washing/laundry		
(e) family shopping		

18. Are any of these domestic tasks shared with other family members (e.g. husband, older children, parents etc)?
Please specify who it is that helps you in each task.

	Regularly	Occasionally	Never
Childcare			
Preparing meals			
Housework			
Washing/laundry			
Family shopping			

19. Do you have any paid or unpaid non-family help with any of these tasks? Please give brief details.

20. Do you have any areas of farm work which are primarily your responsibility?

    YES / NO → if yes, please give brief details.

21. Which of the following farm activities are you involved in? (tick as appropriate)

	Regularly	Occasionally	Emergency only	Never
(a) office work/book-keeping				
(b) dealing with callers/ telephone calls				
(c) running errands for the business				
(d) manual farm work (e.g. feeding animals)				
(e) helping at harvest time				
(f) dealing with employees				
(g) providing accommodation for employees				
(h) providing meals for employees				
(i) day-to-day management decisions				
(j) long-term management decisions				
(k) farm shop/gate sales				
(l) bed and breakfast accommodation				
(m) commercial horse-riding activities				

22. How many hours per week (roughly, on average) would you say that you put into the activities you have listed in questions 20 and 21 above?

    (a) Hours per week.

    (b) As a proportion of total FAMILY labour (i.e. all the hours worked by your FAMILY on the farm, including your husband).

    less than ¼   ¼ to ½   more than ½

23. Does your involvement in these activities change in type or amount on a seasonal basis? Please give brief details.

(ibid., pp.152–3)

Passage 10.2

Up at 7.30, put the kettle on and make tea, go out to fetch the cows in for morning milking, mix calf milk and feed the calves, take a cup of tea out to Tom [in the milking parlour]. Feed the yearlings in the yard and bed out the horses and feed them. Feed the poultry. Get the break-fast [for her husband, herself and usually her daughter] for about 9.00. Clear away, do some washing, think about what to make for lunch. Make lunch for about 1.00. Clear up, hang out the washing. Go out to help shift the sheep, I'm used as a stationary gate. Back to the house, make the beds and do the bathroom then its really whatever turns up, there's always some 'rep' [sales representative for an inputs firm] turning up or something and I'm the first line of defence, it's my job to keep them away from Tom [husband] unless he's said otherwise. Make the fires up in time for everyone coming in to tea. 4.30 have tea, usually make a cake, everyone comes in for that [usually husband, daughter and son-in-law]. After tea I fetch the cows in again for after-noon milking [daughter does the milking] and feed the calves and bed the horses. Make tea for about 6.00 [supper]. Clear up and then go and sit by the fire in the back room until bed, about 9.30.
(ibid., p.88)

11

Women's Paid Work Inside the Home

Sheila Allen and Carol Wolkowitz (1987), *Homeworking: myths and realities*, Basingstoke, Macmillan.

Mariam Fraser

Homeworking

Working from home is increasing. Lack of outside employment which can be fitted around childcare and other responsibilities forces many people, especially women, to take waged work into the home. This is usually low-paid and sometimes even dangerous. Yet, despite the importance of homework to many women's lives and work experience, and to the wider economy more generally, it is an area which has largely been ignored. This is because sociology has traditionally concentrated on waged work outside the home or unpaid domestic labour inside the home.

By drawing on women's experiences, Allen and Wolkowitz examine the way homeworking fits around women's responsibilities and provides a vital contribution to the family income. They reveal that homeworking is not a convenient way to earn some extra cash ('pin money') over and above a (male) wage but is in fact a 'real job' done under very poor conditions.

The authors also show how homeworking benefits the general economy. Struggling businesses, in an effort to increase profits, often transfer many of their costs (such as lighting, heating, equipment) onto the individual homeworker. The women who work from home are in no position to fight for better rights and conditions, given their dependence on the homeworking wage.

Homeworking: myths and realities, by examining the nature of homeworking (both past and present), the assumptions made about homeworking, and the degree to which homeworking is not a rare form of labour but rather an integral part of the wider economy, dispels many of the myths perpetuated by male models of work and production.

Research Design

Allen and Wolkowitz initially examined official statistics to gain a rough estimate of the number of homeworkers in Britain. They concluded that these were inaccurate, due to the inadequacy of definitions and the inappropriateness to women's experience in the labour force of classifications based on men's working lives. Problems also included the reluctance both to admit to working from home (particularly for those receiving unemployment benefits or working illegally from council houses) and to recognize work from home as 'real' work.

In their own empirical research, based in West Yorkshire, the authors initially made contact with homeworkers through personal introductions. They later conducted a door-to-door survey using women with local backgrounds and accents to knock on the doors (to reduce suspicion about the reasons for data collection on homeworking). 4190 households were surveyed, 48% of these had someone at home, among whom 115 homeworkers were found. One of the problems with Allen and Wolkowitz's research is that they do not specify exactly how many homeworkers they interviewed, or why these women particularly were chosen (see *Critical Observations*, p.123).

The authors carried out a content analysis of advertisements for homeworking in 18 local papers and in Job Centres. Information about who supplied homeworking was also given by homeworkers and ex-homeworkers. Overall, 88 firms were identified from different industries (see *Table 11.1*, p.125). Interviews were also carried out with agents, middlemen, employees and ex-employees of firms supplying homework, and with trade union officials.

Allen and Wolkowitz's research suggested that official estimates of the number of homeworkers was too low. They estimate the number of homeworkers to be between 1% and 2.6% of those officially recorded as economically active.

Principal Findings

(i) *Types of homeworking*

Despite the popular view that homeworking is based around the garment industry or done by immigrant entrepreneurs and their kinship networks, homeworkers in West Yorkshire were undertaking a wide variety of work. Much of the work was highly skilled, and if it was not, this was not necessarily due to the homeworkers' lack of skill, but because the conditions that led her to undertake homeworking often meant giving up skilled employment outside of the home. Homeworking ranged from sewing, knitting and hand-crafting, to assembling parts previously hand- or machine-worked in factories; these included joining nuts to bolts, covering fireworks and assembling sample cards. Packing and packaging were also common, including activities like washing, sorting, trimming, collating, bagging, stapling, labelling and sealing. Work might involve the production of whole articles from raw materials or partial production of goods.

'New' technologies, often related to computer data-processing, were also found. Although relatively well-paid compared to the more conventional types of homeworking (because the workers command scarce skills), Allen and Wolkowitz argue that these jobs may not be so profitable in the future.

> It is as well to remember that 'new' technology has always been a part of homeworking production. The sewing machine and the typewriter . . . were once new technologies. Their adoption did not lead to new relations of production between supplier and worker, or employee and employer. (Allen and Wolkowitz, 1987, p.55)

(ii) *Socio-economic groupings*

Using several different labour market indicators, Allen and Wolkowitz conclude that over three quarters of the households doing homeworking fell into the manual/working class bracket. However, many of these women had had white collar experience before having children, making them downwardly mobile on becoming mothers. All but three of the homeworkers interviewed said that their earnings went towards basic necessities such as heating, food, rent or mortgage repayments.

(iii) *Reasons for homeworking (including the differences between Pakistani and white women)*

The authors found that having dependent children was only one factor amongst many for homeworking:

> . . . such constraints are used to justify the construction of women as an appropriate labour force and to legitimate a method of production which persists primarily because of its benefits to employers. (ibid., p.183)

Most women continued homework while their children were very young and 25 women entered homeworking during their 30s and 40s.

With the exception of one Pakistani woman who worked at home for religious reasons, the other ten Pakistani homeworkers interviewed cited the same reasons as white women for doing homework (childcare and economic need). Although only the families of 50 respondents had explicitly insisted that the women should stay at home, the authors argue that women are often under familial pressure not to go out to work, whether this is clearly articulated or not.

The majority of Pakistani women had previously worked outside the home; only three were wary of this, or lacked sufficient knowledge of English to do so. Allen and Wolkowitz conclude that the determination of the Pakistani women's work options were similar to those of white women and not as simple as the 'housebound Asian woman' myth implies.

Additionally, none of the Pakistani women were employed by their own relatives and over half were employed by white bosses. The only real difference noted between white and Pakistani homeworkers was that, contrary to popular opinion, there was often a tradition of home-working in white women's families. Allen and Wolkowitz acknowledge that Pakistani women face prejudice in the labour market, which contributes to the decision to undertake homework, but argue that they share the same problems that face all women in the work force.

(iv) *Hours, pressures and pay*

The majority of homeworkers in the study worked similar hours to those outside the home in part-time jobs (11–30 hours), although three worked over 40 hours per week. Work was not undertaken for short periods, but was considered to be a continuing source of employment. 16 women had taken on homeworking in addition to jobs outside the home.

Working at home stereotypically conjures up images of a less stressful day, easier time-management and an ability to fit work around domestic chores. Some think homeworking, with these advantages, will replace 'proper jobs' in the future. Allen and Wolkowitz strongly dispute this. During their survey they found that although homeworkers do not have the pressure of a supervisor or clocking in and out of work, fixed delivery times and payment by the piece effectively controlled their hours and their pace. Piece-rate work requires speed and efficiency which is difficult to build up if the type of work changes as often as weekly. Homeworkers are dependent on the supplier for the work and often have too little or too much. In the latter instance, they still have to meet the suppliers' deadlines to receive payment. They rarely refused work and were not paid for holidays or sick leave

The authors argue that the assumption that the home is a place of relief from work only applies to men. For women, the responsibility for domestic chores and family care turns all homes into workplaces. This is exacerbated for homeworkers who have no spatial separation between their paid and unpaid labour. Family members do not adjust their expectations to the homeworker's needs (which may be one reason why it is encouraged by partners and children). Husbands and children often worked with the mother, although this was carefully negotiated and in several instances the family were paid for their help thus lowering the mother's own earnings further. Pay for homeworking varied, but all the wages were low.

> Over one-quarter of the 72 homeworker households fell below the Low Pay Unit definition of low pay for 1980. (ibid., p.68)

One woman sewed and knitted horse blankets for 75p each, which were then sold for £20 in shops. Homeworkers rarely receive reimbursement for expenses from suppliers and neither can they claim money back through the tax system (see *Passage 11.2*, p.126).

The Economic Context of Homeworking

Allen and Wolkowitz situate their analysis of homeworking within the more general constraints in which women's paid work is conducted:

> Homeworking is a particularly appalling example of women's position in the labour market, not a contrast to it. (ibid., p.85)

This approach avoids stereotyping women homeworkers as (a) house-wives/mothers (dependent on a male wage); (b) exceptionally desperate and forced to accept low wages; or (c) doing homeworking for 'pin-money'. Instead, the authors argue that homeworkers face the same problems as women who work outside the home – as economic contributors to the household and as life-long carers for children, the elderly and the sick. Yet lack of work options in the labour-market, and the 'naturalness' of women as carers is rarely questioned.

> If there were adequate public child-care facilities, or more jobs outside the home to suit those responsible for dependants, homeworkers' 'choice' of work might be very different. (ibid., p.73)

Additionally, they note that although homeworking is low paid, outside of the home one out of three or four workers is also low paid.

The association of women's homeworking and its casual character only replicates the conventional view of women's paid work as being of secondary importance. Despite the vital contribution of homeworking to the family income, it is ignored in dominant constructions of the labour force;

> Explaining homeworking in terms of the characteristics of homeworkers mistakes cause for effect. It leaves out of the analysis the social divisions and social processes through which the labour force is constructed and differentially allocated to jobs which command different levels of remuneration and different conditions of work. (ibid., p.183)

Allen and Wolkowitz argue that theoretical frameworks which try to explain homeworking by looking at *homeworkers' preferences* are misleading. Such approaches, they argue, give a false view because they imply that it is suitable for the homeworker, instead of observing how she is exploited for the benefit of the employer:

> The distinctive gender composition of the homeworking labour force in Britain has led investigators to explain homeworking in terms of its advantages to 'housewives' who are constrained from accepting other forms of employment. ... [M]ost explanations of women's position in the labour-market invoke women's 'dual role' as an explanation of women's

segregation in low-paid jobs and the expansion of part-time employment
for women. . . . In contrast, comparatively little attention is devoted to
the organisation of women's paid labour by employers to suit their own
priorities. (ibid., p.88)

They found that homeworking was not a form of petty commodity
production, but rather a method of production used by both large and
small scale capitalist enterprises. One of the reasons for this is the
expanding global economy which enables multi-national corporations
to utilize cheap labour in developing countries. Homeworking can cut
costs for UK firms by putting the risks and costs of production,
normally borne in factories and offices, onto the homeworker. These
include overhead costs (lighting, heating, work space) as well as costs
of recruitment, supervision and management. The lack of employment
contracts (and therefore employment rights) enables the firm to pay
low wages and give few benefits. This also provides a 'flexible' labour
force to whom there are no long-term responsibilities. The authors
see similarities between homeworking (as a form of relocation of
production) and the increasing casualization of out-working
employees' terms and conditions. They note the high incidence of
temporary contracts, which lead to worse employment conditions and
fewer benefits. They argue that these similarities should be viewed as
a symptom of, and not a solution to, the economic recession.

Other methods of cutting costs without reducing control include
the externalization and decentralization of production. This may occur
through subcontracting to smaller companies (who then bear the
brunt of risk-taking), through privatization (for example, the public
sector putting out work to private companies thus by-passing trade
unions and decreasing wages), and through neo-familialism. Neo-
familialism is

> based on the notion that the family's role in reproduction can be extended
> into areas previously located in the market sphere. (ibid., p.175)

Thus families would become 'self-provisioning' – that is, they would
provide goods and services for themselves and might exchange these
with other families without entering into the market place. Allen and
Wolkowitz show how this has already started:

> Cuts in social services and welfare benefits, reinforced by the ideology
> of community care, assume that families will care for the sick, handi-
> capped elderly, and will support young people . . . (ibid., p.176)

This particularly affects women whose paid and unpaid labour is
already stretched to its limits. Neo-familialism would also have
repercussions in the wider economy. For example, there would be less
demand for goods and services that families currently use and, as a
result, the government would be deprived of revenue from taxation.

The authors review the advantages and disadvantages of Wages Councils, trade unions, local homeworking groups, etc., and examine what these groups are doing to improve the situation of homeworkers as well as what they will potentially be able to do in the future. Their own short-term practical recommendations include:

(a) that homeworkers be recognized as waged workers, not as self-employed;
(b) that the responsibility of the employer should be recognized;
(c) legislation covering and monitoring homeworking;
(d) that homeworkers have better employment status and at least a minimum wage.

In the longer term, Allen and Wolkowitz advocate,

[c]hanges not only in the sexual division of labour but in the power relations between men and women [and] in the division between public and private responsibilities. (ibid., p.189)

Critical Observations

Allen and Wolkowitz's book was one of the first to tackle the complex questions raised by homeworking and, as such, broke new ground in the debates around work and women's lives. However, critics have pointed out some unwarranted assumptions.

Firstly, the authors have ignored work done by black women on homeworking. Julia Burdett (1988) argues that although Allen and Wolkowitz recognize the racism endemic in British society, they do not explore fully the specific effects of this on black homeworkers:

This dismissiveness fails fundamentally to comprehend the race dimension which informs the complex analytical framework within which black and minority ethnic women researchers work in Britain, and appears to imply that elements of their research can have no application for women in the white majority community. (Burdett, 1988, p.269)

Secondly, Hilary Silver (1988) argues that the authors' views *assume* that any desire on the part of women to stay at home is a result of false consciousness (reflected in the authors' suggested policy proposals which aim to get women out of the home) which simplifies women's complex reasons for homeworking. One of these reasons may be a genuine wish to work at home.

Thirdly, Silver criticises the authors' analysis of social class. She points out that because some homeworkers own their means of production, perform management functions and hire other homeworkers (Silver, 1988, p.298), their position as 'disguised wage workers', as described by Allen and Wolkowitz, hides the contradictions in homeworkers' class position.

Finally, there have been reservation about Allen and Wolkowitz's methodology. It is unclear how many homeworkers Allen and

Wolkowitz interviewed – the figure varies (between 71 and 90) throughout the book. Nor is it clear how the areas that Allen and Wolkowitz researched were chosen, nor why those interviewed were selected from all the homeworkers who were identified. Additionally, the authors make generalizations about the whole of Britain based on the West Yorkshire area, which may in fact have a higher incidence of homeworking, given the unemployment in this area.

Conclusion

Despite these criticisms, Allen and Wolkowitz highlight an important but under-researched area of women's lives; chapter 5 provides some moving examples of what homeworking involves for women and their families. For example, they note how rarely homeworkers ever refuse work, and when they do, it is usually because they are ill. They also show how the pressure from suppliers of homeworking becomes an unquestioned part of life which most in-workers would find totally unacceptable.

Allen and Wolkowitz draw together many of the debates around homeworking and, most importantly, show how the demands made on women by their families and society actually work to the benefit of the wider economy. These demands are seen to be 'natural' for women and, therefore, are rarely questioned. However, they argue that it is this hidden ideology that perpetuates conditions which force women to accept work that is low-paid and unfulfilling. Allen and Wolkowitz emphasise that the advantages of homeworking to the employer should be recognized and that basic assumptions about homeworking should be reformulated. This alternative analysis promises more effective ways to improve the conditions of homeworkers.

Bibliography and Further Reading

Burdett, J. (1988), Review of 'Home-based work in Britain' (London, Department of Employment (1987), by Catherine Hakim) in *Work, Employment and Society*, Vol. 2, No. 2, June 1988, pps.268–269.

Feminist Review (1986) *Waged Work – A Reader*, London, Routledge. (especially 'Homeworking and the control of women's work' by Sheila Allen and Carol Walkowitz, pps.238–265)

Jenson, J. *et al.* (1988), *Feminisation of the Labour Force*, Cambridge, Polity Press.

Leicester Outwork Campaign – 'Annual Reports'.

Rowbotham, S. (1993), *Homeworking Worldwide*, London, Merlin Press.

Rowbotham, S. and Mitter, S. (eds.) (1994), *Dignity and Daily Bread*, London, Routledge.

Silver, Hilary (1988) Review of 'Homeworking: Myths and Realities' in *Sociology*, Vol. 22, No. 2, pps.298–299.

Walby, Sylvia (ed.)(1988), *Gender, Segregation and Work*, Oxford, OUP (especially 'Gender, Racism and Occupational Segregation' by A. Phizacklea).

West Yorkshire Low Pay Group (1990), *A Penny a Bag*, Batley, Yorkshire and Humberside Low Pay Unit.

Westwood, S. and Bhachu, P. (1988), *Enterprising Women*, London, Routledge.

Appendices

Table 11.1 – Suppliers of homework, 1980[a]

Industries (SIC classification)	No. of firms using homeworkers[b]		
	West Yorks	Bradford	Total
Food, drink, tobacco	1	1	2
Chemical & allied industries	4	3	7
Textiles	4	4	8
Clothing and footwear	12	9	21
Paper, printing & publishing	5	5	10
Other manufacturing industries	7	6	13
Distributive trades	7	4	11
Insurance, banking & finance	1	1	2
Professional and scientific services	1	1	2
Total	42	34	76

[a] Named firms only
[b] Twelve firms identified were based outside the West Yorkshire and Metropolitan District of Bradford area.
(Allen and Wolkowitz, 1987, Table 2.4, p.47)

Passage 11.1 Introduction to the Policy adopted by the 1984 National Conference on Homeworking.

Homeworkers' Charter
The demands contained in this Charter are those made by home-workers. The vast majority are women who suffer the triple burdens of childcare, housework and employment. Homeworkers are caught in the poverty trap and as such provide cheap, unorganised labour, especially for the sectors of industry which perpetuate the worst employment practices. Homeworking, especially in the new tech-nology industries, both in manufacturing and the provision of services, is on the increase; it is now being promoted as the way of working in the future even by multinational concerns. It is clear that the bad employment practices of traditional industries are being imported into the newer ones to the detriment of worker organisation. Homeworkers, who are particularly vulnerable to racist and sexist exploitation, subsidise their employers' profits and there is no doubt that given better opportunities few homeworkers would work at home.
(ibid., Appendix A.2, p.195)

Passage 11.2 On the difficulties homeworkers face in claiming expenses for tax purposes and one homeworkers' testimony before the Select Committee in 1981

Many homeworkers earn below the tax threshold, and are therefore unable to reclaim expenses in the form of tax rebates. In [one home-worker's] case, however, the firm which supplied her work withdrew tax, but she did not reclaim the extra £3.50 a week on her electricity bill. Nor had she been able to obtain adequate advice from tax officials about her other expenses. At the end of her testimony she came back with a question:

> 'As far as tax rebates are concerned for certain things, do they [the tax inspectors] have the right at different offices to turn round and say: "Look, that's your choice, that's your problem", because I do not say I would claim for carpets but I go through a carpet a year. . . . So I have to pay out money to buy that once a year. I shampoo and shampoo it till it is threadbare [to get rid of the industrial waste] but there are other things you have to consider – the fact you are using electricity. I have to buy tools. I have to have my scissors sharpened and my scissors in particular are very expensive. I pay £4 a pair for good scissors which you have to have'.

(ibid., pp.96–97).

12

Migration, its Reasons and Outcomes

Vaughan Robinson (1986), *Transients, Settlers and Refugees*, Oxford, Clarendon Press.

John Hartley

Introduction

Transients, Settlers and Refugees looks at the migration to Britain of both South and East African Asians and in so doing, uses Blackburn, Lancashire, as a case study. It groups Black settlements in Britain into types sharing common characteristics, and uses this typology in order to anticipate the migrants' life chances – that is, the opportunities and constraints which they will experience in British society. It goes on to look at the actual process of migration and the forces both *pushing* them from the sending areas and *pulling* them towards the receiving areas in Britain. The study then examines the structural and cultural forces affecting both groups and provides models to show how Asian migrants fit into British society. Hypotheses are then drawn from these models and empirically tested using the results of a 'specially commissioned survey of an entire Asian community'.

Much of the previous work on ethnic minorities in Britain has been in the form of community studies which, although very revealing about the specific community under examination, have been criticized for not leading to any general or universal patterns. Vaughan Robinson has brought interdisciplinary methods to bear on this question, and attempts to blend 'the particular with the universal' – that is, to generalize out from a particular study and create theoretical explanations, whilst appreciating specific local outcomes. He draws on earlier work on migration by Ballard and Ballard (1977), Smith (1977) and Brown (1984), concepts of housing classes from Rex and Moore (1967), and closure, encapsulation, and marginality from Parkin (1979), Mayer (1961), and Park (1928). This work is a mixture of sociology, geography, anthropology, and history. It fits within the traditions of the sociology of race, British race relations, the geography of race relations, and social and human geography.

Research Design

Data was collected in two stages, the 1977 Asian Census and, a year later, the 1978 Sample Survey.

The 1977 Asian Census gathered information from doorstep interviews of 1,702 households in Blackburn. This represents 77% of those approached and provided information on 4,721 adults and 4,141 children. The sample frame used was the electoral roll plus a further 97 families, who were not on the electoral roll but were contacted by snowball interviewing – that is, by asking respondents if they knew of any Asian families not on the electoral roll, and who were then interviewed. The questionnaire contained 'only those questions needed to derive social and demographic data and was designed intentionally to minimize the length of the interview and therefore maximize the response rate.' (Robinson, 1986, p.209)

The 1978 Sample Survey collected more in-depth information of both a quantitative and qualitative nature. The sample fraction was determined simply by available time. The sample frame was the 1978 Blackburn Electoral Roll. 500 households were contacted, resulting in pre-arranged interviews at 391 of them – a 78% response rate – representing approximately 18% of Asian households on the Electoral Roll. An interview schedule was employed which contained 185 questions, of which '138 were pre-coded, the remainder being structured discussions.'

In both surveys, interviewees were contacted in advance by letter which also explained the aims of the survey. The interviewers were chosen partly because of the languages they spoke: in Robinson's words they were carefully matched 'with the regional-linguistic characteristics of those Asians known to live in a particular area'.

Principal Findings

The aim of the study was to test an abstract model 'designed to elucidate the position of Asian immigrants in British society' (see *Figure 12.1*, p.137 for the model) by investigating four specific issues:

(i) Whether different reasons for *being* in Britain led to different orientations once here
(ii) Whether Asian immigrants may objectively be regarded as an underclass
(iii) Whether South Asians are *encapsulated* and East African Asians *marginalized*
(iv) The level of assimilation/desegregation *within* the South Asian and East African Asian population

(i) *Different orientations: transients, settlers, or refugee?*

Robinson demonstrates that there are differences in the reasons why different Asian groups came to Britain and goes on to argue that this may alter their orientation, both towards the indigenous population and to other Asian groups. (See *Table 12.1*, p.136 for the reasons given for migration to Britain by Asian interviewees in the 1978 sample survey.)

Examination of East African Asian migration showed that, rather than there being an economic or voluntary impetus, the movement was 'compulsory, politically induced, and unplanned'. The main reason for migration given by East African Asians was 'political problems'. Robinson also points out that the East African Asians had experienced a higher status position in their society than had South Asians, and he argues that this led to higher expectations for themselves within British society.

With regard to South Asian migration, Robinson stresses the importance of economic motives in the decisions of those coming from India and Pakistan. He argues that both the type and locality of housing which South Asians might choose, or have access to, could also be affected by these motives. The reason given for migrating to Britain by almost half of those questioned was associated with employment and over 20% said they had friends and relatives here.

For South Asians there were powerful *push* factors. One example of these was the pressure on the land due to a high density of population and the partitioning of India in 1947, when there were massive movements of population between India and Pakistan. Other examples include specific local issues such as the building of the Mangla Dam in the early 1960s, which led to around 100,000 Mirpuris being displaced and given compensation, used by some to come to Britain looking for work.

There were also strong *pull* factors, such as the tradition of overseas migration and the strength of the British economy at the time, and therefore the possibility of comparatively high wages. Robinson states that most authors agree that this combination of factors produced mass migration, but that there is no agreement as to their relative importance. He maintains that

> the cultural ethos which underpins the sending society is more important than the specific motives behind migration. The sending society is characterized by a search for improved status or honour (izzet) which is equated with material wealth. (ibid., p.27)

Once they have arrived in Britain, Robinson argues that 'the two main groups (South Asians and East African Asians) are likely to adopt different roles in British society because of their contrasting migration histories.' During the early stages of migration, the South Asian migrants were mainly economically active males. Their intention was to increase the social position of their families in South Asia by sending

money back to them. They viewed their stay in Britain as temporary
and believed that they would return 'home' one day.

Up until 1956 92% of all Pakistanis/Bangladeshis who had come to
Britain were males. By 1974 that figure was still 65% and the amount
of money known to have been sent to Pakistan by Pakistanis in Britain
rose from £19.77 million in 1973 to £67.76 million in 1983.

By contrast, East African Asian migrants prior to 1967 were mainly
young single men, predominantly from wealthy families. They had
come to Britain either to enter higher education or to investigate the
possibility of the whole family migrating. The later arrivals were
mainly shopkeepers and clerks who were anticipating a forced
migration from Uganda and consisted of whole families, both male and
female, of a wider age range, not just the young. With the expulsion
of Ugandan Asians in 1972, refugees came from a complete mixture of
social classes and ages and tended to be in extended family groups.
Robinson points out that this gives them a 'unique character' as
migrants, for the South Asian migrants have few elderly dependents
in Britain.

(ii) An underclass?

The study focusses largely on the issue of housing to investigate the
effects of structural and cultural forces on the Asian population in
Blackburn and in Britain as a whole. It investigates whether it is
objectively possible to regard all Asians as a deprived underclass
excluded both from an equal participation in society and from a share
of its scarce resources. Richardson and Lambert (1985) define an
underclass as

> a disadvantaged group which does not share the same experiences or
> privileges as the white working class. . . . leading a 'marginalised'
> existence since they have not yet been fully incorporated into traditional
> working class organisations (such as trade unions and the labour party).

Robinson concludes that 'regardless of whether one looks purely at the
issue of housing or takes a more general view, Asians are a deliberately
excluded and disadvantaged group. In this respect Rex's conceptualiza-
tion of Asians and other coloured groups in Britain as an underclass
is fully supported' (ibid., p.202).

The relationship between Blackburn's Asian population and the
indigenous white one is examined and 'the way in which Asians are
viewed by Blackburnians, young and old, working and middle class' is
illustrated by using quotes from Blackburnians taken from Jeremy
Seabrook's City Close Up (1971). Robinson points out that the most
obvious point arising from these comments is that the immigrants are
perceived as a threat. In the Blackburn Council Elections in 1976, the
National Party (extreme right wing) received 1,588 votes in one ward,
and as a consequence two of their members became councillors: 'the
first elected representatives of their party in Britain' (ibid., p.129).

Robinson argues for the importance of the housing issue stating that, both nationally and locally, there are racial attitudes towards housing access.

> White society persistently and systematically places barriers in the way of those coloured immigrants who wish to gain access to better housing in better residential neighbourhoods. (ibid., p.199)

Figures for housing tenure in 1977 in Blackburn showed that 94% of Asians owned their own homes (the national figure was 72%) rather than renting them. Many Asians had low incomes or insecure employment which effectively debarred them from the traditional mortgage/bank loan market. Of the sample interviewed in Blackburn in 1978, only 6.6% of owner occupiers were using building societies to buy their houses. They therefore turned to cheaper, inner city, housing, 32% buying outright using joint family resources and 26% obtaining mortgages from the local authority under a special scheme aimed at low income families.

Robinson suggests that there was discrimination from both estate agents and house vendors and that this altered the 'search behaviour' of the Asian population of Blackburn when they were looking for a new house. The study states that 34% relied on friends and relations, 19% were informed by informal/private advertisements, 21% saw properties advertised in (Asian) shops, and 2% in local newspapers. If an estate agent *was* used he might in fact be Asian. Striking cases of anti-Asian feeling are described, the most vivid being '23 year old Graham Jones who lived in Norwich Street in Blackburn. When he decided to sell his house he erected a *For whites only* sign beneath the *For Sale* notice' (ibid., p.137). Whatever the method used to examine the issue of housing it is obvious that there is a spatial separation between the Asian population and the indigenous one.

The study argues that 'exclusionary closure' *is* practised against the Asian population but that different Asian groups may react differently to this. This exclusion takes the form of 'prejudice, discrimination, calls for a reduction in immigration, changes in voting behaviour, and social avoidance' (ibid., p.113). However, even though the indigenous population sets up these boundaries, there is a variety of reactions to them within the Asian population. For example, many South Asian groups attempt to maintain their own culture and keep themselves relatively isolated and therefore many of the exclusionary practices affect them far less than the East African Asians.

Having looked at the structural forces in operation, the study also examines the cultural ones and argues that

> although the evidence suggests that, objectively, Asians are confined to the inner areas of Blackburn from whence it is difficult for them to escape, this perhaps ignores a preference on their part for neighbourhoods of this type . . . When asked why they lived in the area where they did, not one respondent in the 1978 Sample Survey mentioned the lack of alternatives. (ibid., p.140)

This perhaps shows that there may be an internal (cultural) desire to live in the inner city areas as well as an external (racist) pressure. The close proximity of relatives was the most popular reason for inter-viewees living where they did (28%), then came the closeness of the mosque (20%), followed by the type and price of housing (12%), then attractiveness of the area (11%), and finally the nearness of friends (11%).

There is an argument within British race relations that the Black and Asian population of Britain belong to an underclass – that is that they are excluded (as described above) from other social classes. Rex and Moore (1967) put forward the idea of 'housing classes' and illustrated, via the issue of housing, that some migrant groups are effectively excluded from certain scarce resources. Robinson uses this notion to illustrate how the exclusion from this one resource 'crystal-lizes attitudes and has a direct bearing on the overall view which society holds of a particular migrant group' (ibid., p.66).

However, the study argues that whilst it may be the case that most of the Black and Asian population of Britain could be seen as belonging to this housing class or underclass, that does *not* mean that they share common interests or a common identity. Robinson suggests that migrant groups need to be viewed individually in terms of their aspira-tions and expectations. Only then will we have a full understanding of the variety of ethnic groups within Britain.

(iii) *Encapsulated or marginalized?*

The pre-migrational experiences of South Asians and East African Asians in Britain, their reasons for coming here, and their attitudes towards permanent residence, were all shown to differ between the two groups. The results of the surveys led Robinson to describe the South Asians as *encapsulated* and the East African Asians as *marginalized*. (see *Figure 12.1*, p.137)

The study argues that for the first generation of South Asian migrants there was a feeling of 'transience' – that is, their stay here was expected to be only temporary. Added to this, they were not attracted to 'the British way of life' and they therefore began to protect and strengthen their own culture, creating what Robinson describes as a 'self-contained satellite' of South Asian society within Britain.

The result of this self-imposed separation was to produce what has been described as 'the myth of return' – that is a belief, amongst first generation South Asians, that there will be a return migration once they have succeeded in their objectives within Britain. The study argues that although this belief is changing through the second and third generations, it still creates 'a mentality towards life in Britain the effects of which are far-reaching and long-lasting' (ibid., p.98). The South Asian minority in Blackburn are shown to have restricted aspirations within Britain. Partly because of the myth of return and their wish to send money to their families in South Asia, they do not wish to become fully involved in British society. If this is added to the structural constraints imposed by the indigenous population, it has ensured 'that the group remains encapsulated in its neighbourhood of residence, in its place of work, and in its place of learning' (ibid., p.176).

However, this argument applies only to South Asian migrants and *not* to those coming to Britain from East Africa. These migrants had *no* myth of return.

> The East African Asian was more concerned with finding and exploiting vacant or undersubscribed economic niches in Britain as he had done in Africa. If this necessitated interaction with the indigenous population then this occurred, as did the adoption of more Westernized traits and outlooks when this was advantageous. The East African must not therefore be thought of as an embattled transient fighting to defend each and every element of his culture and identity. (ibid., p.98)

East African Asian groups faced the same type of exclusionary barriers as South Asians but, the study argues, they were much more aware of them. Because of the status that they had enjoyed in East Africa, their expectations of life and ambitions for social and financial mobility were higher than those of South Asians. The study concludes that the fact that they had internalized many Western values but were still barred from inclusion in British society 'was likely to leave them in a marginal social position' (ibid., p.204).

(iv) *The level of assimilation within the two groups*

Level of assimilation is the *extent* to which the migrant groups have become part of British society or have remained separate. Robinson states that the single most important point resulting from this study is that 'the Asian population' is not one homogeneous group but is in fact 'a series of independent and different sub-communities'. He developed a model of ethnic association in an attempt to describe a continuum 'along which the variety of regional-linguistic groups could be ranged'.

The model of ethnic association

> proposed a series of assimilation phases through which groups might pass on their way to total assimilation, and also indicated the key barriers which might prevent progress from one phase to another. Variables were then selected either as indicants of the phase of assimilation or as surrogates for the barriers. The analysis of these data demonstrates that none of the groups in Blackburn was totally assimilated, and more than this, that no one group was even near to this state. However, the groups could be arranged along a continuum of ethnic association and their level of relative assimilation identified. The results indicated that the more assimilated groups tended to be East Africans, whilst the South Asians remained intent upon encapsulatory closure. (ibid., pp.201–2)

By 'encapsulatory closure', Robinson means that the South Asians have kept themselves enclosed, both socially and culturally.

The study concludes that this encapsulatory closure, fuelled by the myth of return, appears to be a far stronger determinant of South Asian behaviour and mobility than the exclusionary barriers. Robinson claims that this finding runs counter to current academic and government beliefs that assimilation (or integration) is *desired* by all Black and Asian groups in Britain. Further, he takes issue with the desirability of policies designed to enforce such integration.

Critical Observations

Many previous studies of minority groups in Britain have concentrated on one particular town or city and have been purely descriptive in nature. Accounts have looked at such things as housing (Rex and Moore, 1967), culture (Dahya, 1973), and migration (Ballard and Ballard, 1977). In this work, Vaughan Robinson has attempted a fusion of these issues.

The majority of comments regarding this work were very positive, stating that it goes further than simply summarizing current knowledge regarding Asians in Britain. In his review article, van Amersfoort (1987, p.479) claims that this study surpasses previous ones in two particulars: it tells us both what we *can* and what we cannot learn from a case study and it presents an extremely clear model. In so doing, it 'links the unique with the general and the empirical with the theoretical'.

However, reviewers have also raised several criticisms of the study. Possibly the most serious concerns the discussion of structural forces. Cater (1987, p.469) argues that there is too little coverage of the impact of structural forces, such as the push factors triggering migration, and of theoretical debates on race and class.

Jones (1987, p.621) remarks on the strong conflict theme which is developed in the study and commends the use of theoretical explanations of housing constraints. However both Cater *and* Jones argue that there is too little theoretical discussion regarding migrant labour.

In his review article, Ahmed Gurnah (1988, p.137) argues that Robinson's *structural forces*

> neglect to analyse the State's racist immigration and nationality laws, institutional racism, economic and political deprivation of black working people, gender stereotypes of black women and men, cultural and religious oppressions of their communities, or the discrimination they experience in employment, education and social services.

The question of racism is also discussed by Cater who argues that although Robinson's 'detailed analysis' of the cultural forces is a 'key strength' of the book, his explanations are often internal to the community. For example, 'the defensive position of a black minority in a hostile society and the absence of alternative "choices" is often obscured'. Indeed, Gurnah goes so far as to argue that Robinson 'forces black people out of his account as active political agents with a struggle on their hands'. There is not room here for a discussion of this issue, but it *is* an important one and warrants further consideration. Gurnah actually questions whether the black communities Robinson is describing are the same ones which he has observed and he concludes with the question: 'What is this man doing in my struggle?'

Cater urges caution in the use of some of the findings of this study as the interviews were conducted with first generation heads of household in 1977/8 and it is possible that second generation Asians may react differently.

Conclusion

Transients, Settlers and Refugees provides insight into the motivations of, and constraints on, South Asian and East African Asian groups living in Britain. The study points to the continued importance of the *sending areas* (particularly for South Asians) and the aspirations and expectations stemming from them. For the South Asians the *myth of return* still has some potency but for East African Asians there is no such belief.

A most useful result of the study is the creation of a model of *ethnic association* (see *Figure 12.2*, p.138). Robinson uses the model to demonstrate that there are great differences *between* Asian groups in Britain and that the British Asian population cannot be seen as a homogeneous one.

The study is, as Cater argues, 'not without its flaws', but it remains 'a valuable contribution to research in the geography of race relations'.

Bibliography and Further Reading

van Amersfoort, H. (1987), Review of 'Transients, Settlers, and Refugees' in *Ethnic and Racial Studies Journal*, Vol.10, No.1 pp.478–9.

Anwar, M. (1979), *The Myth of Return*, London, Heinemann.

Cater, J. (1987), Review of 'Transients, Settlers, and Refugees' in *Progress in Human Geography Journal*, Vol.2, pp.468–71.

Gurnah, A. (1988), Review of 'Transients, Settlers, and Refugees' in *Community Development Journal*, Vol.23, No.2, pp.136–8.

Hiro, D. (1992), *Black British White British*, Paladin, London.

Jones, T. (1987), Review of 'Transients, Settlers, and Refugees' in *Contemporary Sociology Journal*, Vol.16, pp.620–1.

Rex, J. and Mason, D. (1986 eds.), *Theories of Race and Ethnic Relations*, Cambridge, Cambridge University Press.

Rex, J. and Moore, R. (1967), *Race, Community, and Conflict*, London, Oxford University Press.

Richardson, J. and Lambert, J. (1985), *The Sociology of Race*, Ormskirk, Causeway Press.

Robinson, V. (1986), *Transients, Settlers, and Refugees*, Oxford, Clarendon Press.

Skellington, R., (1992), *'Race' in Britain Today*, London, Sage.

Werbner, P., (1990), *The Migration Process*, Oxford, Berg.

Appendices

Table 12.1 Stated reasons for migration to Britain

	East African Asians	South Asians
Political problems	31	0
To get a job/career advancement	26	135
Marriage	5	10
Education	11	20
To visit	3	1
Relatives/Friends here	14	61
Sent by parents	1	0
To improve life	13	28
Financial reasons	0	22
Direct recruitment	0	3
Other people coming	0	3
For a change	0	1
Don't know	0	4
Total	104	288

(Robinson, 1986, Table 7.1, p.231)

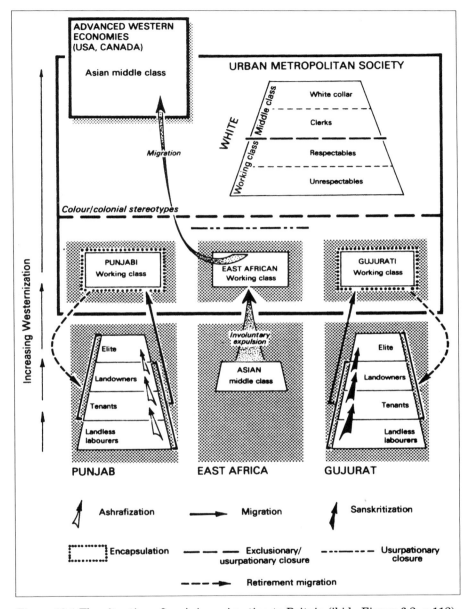

Figure 12.1 The situation after Asian migration to Britain (ibid., Figure 6.2, p.112)

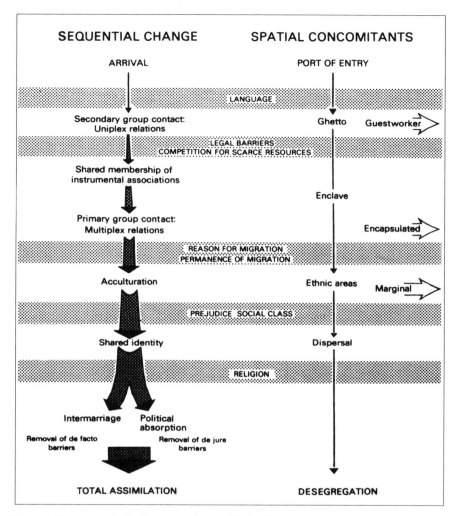

Figure 12.2 A model of ethnic association (ibid., Figure 10.1, p.181)

13

Race and Residence

Susan J. Smith (1989), *The Politics of 'Race' and Residence*, Cambridge, Polity Press.

Ken Hahlo

Introduction

Racism might be regarded less as an historical acquisition, and more 'as a strategy for the future in advanced societies' (Smith, 1989, p.viii). Although Britain has no 'history of domestic slavery or enforced racial separation' (ibid., p.viii), the source of many attitudes and social values associated with racism can be traced back to the British Empire. Today race is one of the chief criteria underlying the system of social stratification in British society. Racism has become a force to be reckoned with in its own right.

This book addresses the theme of racial segregation; it argues that where people live matters. The unequal allocation of scarce resources, such as employment, housing, welfare benefits and education, by local and national post-war governments to black people[1] has created a situation which both reinforces established ideologies of race as well as the importance of social, economic and political processes which underpin racism.

Smith's study combines a conventional with an innovative analysis of the position of black people in Britain. *The Politics of 'Race' and Residence* examines how housing policies, or the lack of them, has affected the position of black people who settled here after the Second World War. Policies which control the distribution of housing are of particular interest since they are a consequence of political decision-making. As some of the social values inherent in this process are racist, politicians have formulated policies on housing that have benefited white people to a greater extent than black people. Thus 'residential

[1] 'Black people' is used to describe Asian and Afro-Caribbean peoples following Smith.

segregation has become a medium for the reproduction of racial inequality' (ibid., p.105). To resolve this situation, she offers four possible solutions.

In developing an explanation, Smith draws upon three sets of ideas: firstly, beliefs which support the exclusiveness of one group over others; secondly, the discriminatory nature of housing and related policies; and thirdly, the politics of race. Two assumptions underpin the notion of exclusiveness: the first rests upon the ideologies of racism and segregationism; the second is the character of the housing policies enacted by those who accept these ideologies. Simply stated, racial ideologies are systems of beliefs which reflect ideas about the superiority or exclusivity of a nation, political system or class over others. A distinction is drawn between racism and segregationism. The former is based on a 'doctrine of biological inequality' (ibid., p.5), but is defined as 'a set of ideas and practices which sustain the notion that races are real and which constructs and reproduces systematic inequalities between the groups so defined' (ibid., p.ix). Segregationism is defined as 'a system of beliefs which seeks justification for racial exclusivity within national boundaries' (ibid., p.6). This encourages people to view black people as 'poor, oppressed and disadvantaged' and thus perpetuates the idea that they are different from white people. In other words racism is made, and therefore it can be countered.

Housing policies reflect an ideological struggle 'over the merits of public versus private ownership' and the targeting of funds for existing and planned projects (ibid., p.50). Therefore, by not recognising a need to provide black immigrants with housing, the Government identified them as a problem. It did this by enacting a range of housing policies which left black people, who were low wage earners, to find housing on the property market. As newly arrived immigrants, and later as tenants or owners, the housing which was available and affordable to buy or rent, was old, dilapidated and in the inner-city. When many of these houses later became the target of slum clearance programmes, they were forced to find alternative accommodation. This meant placing themselves on local authority lists for council housing, looking for affordable privately rented accommodation, or houses to purchase.

While the Government placed the responsibility for creating better housing opportunities for immigrants on local authorities, it made them dependent for resources on national funds. Choosing not to recognize the plight of black people, local authorities allocated housing to those considered to be in the greatest need, namely sections of the white community. As low wage earners, black people could not make use of various subsidies offered by the state to promote home ownership, such as mortgage relief. These subsidies benefited higher wage earners who were mainly white. The implementation of slum clearance programmes favoured those who had lived in their homes the longest and these were not newly arrived black people. With neither central nor local governments being committed to helping them, they became residentially marginalized.

Until the 1980s, Smith argues, residential segregation was the consequence of three strategies: immigration control, race relations legislation and policies intended to achieve desegregation (ibid., p.122). After this, with a new emphasis on the rights of individuals to a good standard of living, government policies stressed the social value of culture rather than race. The Government encouraged black communities to establish their social and cultural identities. Thus the Government could be seen to exchange its support for racial inequality for a commitment to cultural diversity.

Research Design

This study differs from many sociological studies in two respects: firstly, the data are drawn from secondary sources, and secondly, it identifies a problem and offers a solution. It utilizes some of the wealth of data which is being made available for public access. As this body of data is being collected more efficiently than ever before and with a greater awareness of social research methods, it provides exciting new opportunities for research, such as this study of housing. Smith draws her data from such secondary sources, which include censuses, material from the Office of Population Censuses and Surveys and the Central Statistics Office, the Labour Force Survey, House of Commons and other Government publications, Commission for Racial Equality publications and a range of existing studies of black people.

By analyzing the data Smith shows how black people became segregated from white people in British cities. She is able to identify where most black people live, to relate their place of residence to the low value of their houses, to high rates of unemployment, to low rates of social, occupational and political mobility and to greater vulnerability to racial attacks. Her explanations for this pattern of residential separation draw upon a body of local and national Governmental policies. In conclusion she develops a series of possible solutions for improving the position of black people in British society (*Table 13.3*, p.151).

Principal Findings

The aims of this study are: (i) to describe and analyze the extent of residential segregation of black from white people in British cities; (ii) to analyze the political and economic policies of local and national governments which has restricted the housing opportunities available to black people; (iii) to consider the politics of resistance of the black communities to racial segregation and (iv) to offer solutions to this problem.

(i) *Residential segregation*

In the 1980s the black population of Britain accounted for just under
2.5 million (or 3.6%) of the total population. Over half of them describe their origin as South Asian. A quarter describe themselves as
Caribbean (West Indian) with the remaining quarter coming from
Africa, Mediterranean countries and other territories. Some 90% of
these people, as compared to 75% of white people, live within five
major metropolitan areas, namely the South-East, West Midlands,
East Midlands, North-West and Yorkshire/Humberside (*Table 13.1*,
p.149 and *Table 13.2*, p.150). The West Indians were attracted to the
areas where the demand for labour was high in occupations which
white people no longer wished to do (replacement labour). Whereas
the Asians looked for work in contracting industries (supplementary), such as textiles, which were for instance (a) losing women
workers who were not permitted to work night shifts and (b) respond-
ing to the recession by producing more for less cost by employing
Asians, particularly on night shift work. Work opportunities in these
industries attracted black people to cities, such as London,
Birmingham, Bradford, Leeds, Leicester, Manchester and their
surrounding towns. Now about 80% of black people live in the inner
city areas as compared to less than 50% of white people. Half of the
white residents in cities live in neighbourhoods where there are no
black people and 1 in 16 lives in enumeration districts with 5% and
more black people.

The conclusions Smith draws from these statistics are that black
people are more concentrated in metropolitan conurbations and in
inner cities than in small towns or rural areas. The data also show
that in the north Asians are more residentially segregated than Afro-
Caribbeans and white people, while in southern conurbations, Asian
patterns of residence are more similar to those of white people than to
those of Afro-Caribbeans. Underlying the pattern of residential segregation are old and modern processes which divide British cities into
two domains, one black and one white.

Arguably, patterns of residence might promote or restrict social
contact between groups of people. However, there is no simple association between social integration and length or place of residence. An
implication embodied in Government housing policies was that, over
time, black and white people would integrate residentially and by
implication socially, economically and politically. However, some 20 to
30 years of residence here has not brought these ethnic communities
together. Furthermore, the argument that time would reduce social
and cultural differences, and lead to assimilation or integration, has
also proved to be untrue. Segregation of black people has become an
expression of racial inequality arising from (a) their low position in the
labour market; (b) inequalities in the processes of distribution of public
housing, and (c) the combined effect of both of these in restricting their
freedom to purchase or rent housing. Consequently, they have been

confined to poor quality housing in the more densely inhabited inner urban areas.

The social characteristics which identify such areas include high numbers of black people and other immigrants, high numbers living in poverty and ill health, children having low levels of educational achievement, high levels of crime and vulnerability of black people to racial attacks. Firms which once provided work for those living here have closed or moved to areas where they can run more profitably. With these disadvantages black people are more likely than white people to experience unemployment, redundancy and under employment. Thus black people have become trapped in these areas by the low value of their homes and their lack of employment. Spatial separation has become a symbol of their social disadvantage.

(ii) *Housing policies*

According to Smith, 'in Britain, national legislation has been influential in determining the location and quality of black people's housing opportunities, and that this has built the foundations on which racial segregation is erected' (ibid., p.49). After the last war political parties accepted the need for the State to fund public housing on the grounds that such provision was central to the idea of the Welfare State. The 1949 Housing Act made housing available to a much wider number of people in need than just those in the working class. By controlling access to public housing, the Government believed that it could balance the inequalities in income and wealth that are part of a capitalist economy. At that time, however, no attempt was made to link black immigration to housing policies. Without local or national Governmental support, black people's need for housing was not regarded as a priority.

Before 1969 the government believed that the integration of black people could be achieved through housing programmes. For instance, in 1964/65 MPs were told that there was no need to provide housing for immigrants, because they would benefit from the overspill schemes. On the basis of the Housing Repairs and Rents Act (1954), some 160,000–180,000 people per year were relocated to peripheral estates and high rise apartments. By 1969 this view was discounted. The effect of these policies was to restrict opportunities for black people to find housing in the areas that might provide them with opportunities for integration. Few black people had benefited from these programmes. By 1974 only 4% of Asians and 26% of West Indians had been allocated council housing, and most of this was in inner urban areas. Fours years later their allocation had risen to 10% and 50% respectively. Although the government claimed to plan and organize the dispersal of Ugandan Asian refugees who came here in 1972, they could not prevent them settling in areas dominated by Asians. The administrative procedures used by some local authorities to allocate public housing were shown later to be racist; devices such as queueing were used to place black

people at the bottom of housing lists. The housing available to them
for rent and purchase was also the least desired and desirable.

The unequal access of people to housing has become more sharply
defined as the profile of housing sectors has changed over the past 70
years. In 1914 90% of accommodation was privately rented, 10% was
owner occupied and there was no publicly rented housing. 70 years
later the privately rented sector accounted for 9%, the owner occupied
sector for about 63%, and the publicly rented sector for 27%. While
the privately rented sector declined in size as a result of the Rent and
Mortgage (War Restrictions) Act (1915), the other sectors expanded.
The implications of these changes for black people were that, as their
access to publicly rented housing was politically restricted, they
became dependent upon the diminishing privately rented and highly
competitive owner occupied sectors. Although black people had equal
rights with white Britons under the 1948 Nationality Act, they were
less well paid than white workers, and experienced a greater need for
housing. Before 1963 they were disadvantaged by low incomes in the
competition for the purchase of better housing. After this date, the
government introduced a number of housing subsidies which included
tax relief on mortgages. Again black people could not benefit, as most
were low wage earners. Thus the racial disadvantages associated with
being black and a migrant became translated into spatial
segregation.

During the 1970s and 1980s slum clearance, redevelopment and
renewal programmes and the arrival of Ugandan Asian refugees in
different ways intensified this residential separation. Slum clearance
programmes moved white people out of inner city areas into the
suburbs, thus increasing the density of black residents. For instance,
the Housing Acts of 1967, 1971 and 1974 supported a system of
housing allocation which gave more white than black people access to
housing in the suburbs. Redevelopment and renewal programmes
raised the level of the competition between black and white for inner
urban council housing and local authority loans. This made it all the
more important for local authorities to prioritize the applications for
such housing and loans. Thus the racialization of the principles
underlying these procedures only added to the disadvantages
experienced by black people.

Although the urban programme (1968–1977) brought funds to areas
with 'acute needs', these were targeted on areas and not groups. For
instance, between 1970 and 1980 various inner city initiatives were
implemented to reduce racial inequality. Such measures as desig-
nating them General Improvement Areas and Housing Action Areas
did improve facilities for inner city residents. While these programmes
seemed to positively discriminate on behalf of black people, they were
matched by a tightening of immigration controls. Furthermore, the
lack of concern expressed in the 1977 White Paper Policy for the inner
cities and racial discrimination, combined with its administrator's
lack of knowledge, meant that black people were once again not seen

as priorities for support. This White Paper identified black communities as problem communities. However, the access of black people to housing was marginally improved by the development of (a) housing associations, which offered a more flexible form of residence for renting than council housing, and (b) council loans allocated 'down market' on inner urban properties. Nevertheless, these initiatives only extended their residence in older inner city properties. Even though the passing of the 1976 Race Relations Act recognized direct and indirect discrimination, it came too late to protect black communities from the effects of racist allocation of housing.

Between 1953 and 1982 there was a dramatic rise in owner occupation, including an increase in black owner occupation generally and Asian home ownership in particular. After 1982 the government reduced its financial support for public house building, while giving local authority tenants the 'right to buy' their houses. By 1982 72% of Asians and 41% of Afro-Caribbeans owned their homes. Again this seemed to support government policies that encouraged home ownership as a form of investment. However, this occurred at a time when the black communities were experiencing high rates of unemployment and were unable to benefit from the various allocation systems and subsidies that should have improved their general position in British society. Therefore, Smith argues that for the majority of black people home ownership (commodification) did not mean better housing conditions or the possession of an appreciating asset. Furthermore, when people were given the opportunity to buy their council homes, those who could afford to purchase their own homes and benefit from various subsidies were white. A result was that rising numbers of black people were becoming benefit-dependent, trapped and marginalized in the public housing sector. 'There may, then, be a process of racial categorization as well as socio-economic differential dividing those who buy their council houses from those who continue to rent' (ibid., p.63), (residualization). The combined effects of the processes of commodification and residualization on black people has brought about 'economic, social and racial polarisation within and between segments of the housing system' (ibid., pp.64–65) and between white and black.

Initially a policy of dispersal, and later a policy of anti-racism, were seen as appropriate measures to cope with biases in residential segregation. With the government unwilling to define the former and unwilling to commit the resources to the latter, the continued existence of racial segregation appears to condone racism. It points to the existence of institutional racism, that is racism which, consciously and unconsciously, has become a principle underlying governmental decision-making.

(iii) *Politics of resistance*

Smith suggests that economic policies of the welfare state, if anything, have led to a rise in the level of racism. These policies were, and still are, being shaped by past and present political ideas about immigration and race. She identifies three phases. The first, covering the period from 1945/48 to 1958/62, was characterized by the political view that black people would gradually integrate into British society. Evidence of this might be increasing social and residential mobility. However, without positive support for them to integrate, and with politicians stressing the importance of employment for white people, employers gave priority to white applicants, while restricting promotion for black workers. The effect of these measures was to confine them to the 'deteriorating remnants of the privately rented sector and the least attractive portions of owner occupied housing stock' (ibid., p.115). The result was that inner city space became racialized and 'black people were no longer seen as a symbol of post-war regeneration but instead became a symptom of Britain's declining world role' (ibid., p.116).

The second phase, 1958/62 to 1970, was marked by the speed and intensity of the arrival and settlement of immigrants. Racial segregation was linked to three political ideas. Firstly, the idea that the immigration process was the cause of environmental problems in areas where black people settled. Since they did not disperse, they became linked with urban decay. Secondly, the idea that spatial separation and density of settlement could be associated with an increasing demand for resources and services. This supported the image of black people demanding services and benefits at the expense of white people. Thirdly, the idea that the clustering of black people in inner urban areas could be seen as a challenge to white affluence and to white territory. This provided some politicians with the image of white Britons defending themselves against black invaders.

Three strategies were implemented for the purpose of promoting the integration of black people; these were the tightening of immigration controls, the implementation of race relations legislation and measures to ensure desegregation. At governmental levels an emphasis on culture rather than race matched the recognition of social diversity for moral superiority. Black people were now regarded as 'different but equal'. A logical solution was to reduce state control of the market, thereby allowing it to function freely. This, the government believed, would stimulate the economy, which would enable black people to find work and thereby raise their income levels. However the reverse occurred: these solutions exacerbated residential and racial inequalities.

By the third phase, 1970 to 1986, black people had become, for Conservative governments, a symptom of urban malaise linked to a decline in law, order and public morality. Smith claims that the indifference of governments to their needs did more to promote the separation of black from white perspectives than did the resistance of black people to racism. Many of the policies and activities of governments over this period were directed towards containing black people's discontent. Commonsense racism, defined as a public common sense created by politicians, gave credence to the belief that racial segregation is a way of life. In this context Smith argues that as an asset, housing can be used to compete for power. It provides a setting in which householders can define their political identities. The lack of success of black householders to gain power through housing can be measured by the few who have succeeded politically. In cities white people endeavour to control black people through racial discrimination, racial harassment and attack on the streets, in their homes, at school and at work. Though generally black resistance has taken the form of withdrawal rather than confrontation, on occasions the opposite strategy has been used, resulting in rioting and violence. Smith interprets such strategies as evidence of the marginalisation of black people.

Racial segregation of housing is a spatial expression of a society that perpetuates, rather than bridges, differences arising from inequalities in wealth, work and consumption. Drawing on state theory, Smith claims that British society can be regarded as comprising two nations, one black and one white. Thus, racial segregation stands for unequal 'access to some basic rights to citizenship' (ibid., p.181).

(iv) *A resolution*

Racial segregation can be opposed through positive discrimination, commitment to equal opportunities and policies which unite the aims of black and white people. Smith offers four models of intervention for the achievement of racial justice (*Table 13.3*, p.151). In the first two the point of intervention is the individual. The principles of intervention stress the rights of individuals to secure economic efficiency and property rights or to secure universal rights of citizenship. For the first, the means of intervention would take the form of market deregulation; for the second, it would involve state provisioning in cash or kind. The criteria for judging success for the first would be economic prosperity and for the second some evaluation of egalitarianism.

In the third and fourth models the point of intervention is the group. The principle of intervention emphasizes either the general or special needs (technical or structural) of groups. The means of intervention in the third model would take the form of vertical (income) redistribution; in the fourth model it would take the form of horizontal redistribution. This can be separated into coping with age, illness or handicap or compensating for disadvantage and discrimination. To judge the success of the third model 'equality of outcome in material circumstances' would suffice. In the fourth model either 'attainment of minimum standards' or 'attainment of quotas of representation' would be employed. Smith favours the second on the grounds that firstly, 'it tackles the differential distribution of economic, welfare, political and civil rights which . . . are fundamental to the reproduction of racial inequality', and secondly, it stresses the integrity of the individual while eroding the bases of the 'cultural and ideological underpinnings of racial categorization' (ibid., p.196).

Critical Observations

Tim Lee (1990) drew attention to four weaknesses. Firstly, he detected a Marxist undercurrent which reduces the clarity of the arguments. Secondly, debatable points are declared as 'proved' or 'shown', rather than as being suggested. Thirdly, spatial integration, whether as possible or desirable, is given too much weight. Finally, potentially interesting concepts are offered to the reader – such as replacement and supplementary labour, the exchange of ethnicity for culture – but few are explained or used to advantage in the analysis. A similar criticism applies to the usage of 'common sense racism'.

Conclusion

This study adds to our knowledge of racism and housing by drawing attention to the importance of housing as a social, economic and political asset. The role of governments in making and implementing housing policies has led to the residential separation of black from white people. Governmental assumptions on how to manage the integration of black people into British society have been negative and divisive. Consequently, policies have not only not improved their position as low wage earners in low value housing, but have also disadvantaged them in other ways. Unable to achieve social, occupational and political mobility, black people have become trapped within the inner city, where they are seen as a threat to law and order. Today, a solution to their difficulties would need to take some form of economic intervention.

Bibliography

Lee, T. (1990), Review of 'Politics of "Race" and Residence' in *Sociology*, Vol.24, No.2, pp.339–340.
Smith, S.J. (1989), *The Politics of 'Race' and Residence*, Cambridge, Polity Press.

Appendices

Table 13.1 Population distribution in Great Britain 1981–5:[a] percentage of residents in private households

	Total	Black[b]	West Indian[c]	Indian	Pakistani[d]	Bangladeshi[d]	East African[e]
Scotland	9.5 (9.3)	2.1 (1.8)	0.3 (0.0)	2.4 (0.8)	3.4 (5.3)	1.3 (0.0)	1.8
Wales	5.1 (5.1)	1.1 (1.6)	0.6 (0.6)	1.0 (0.9)	1.1 (0.6)	2.1 (2.2)	0.9
North	5.7 (5.7)	1.2 (1.6)	0.2 (0.0)	1.3 (0.7)	2.1 (2.9)	1.6 (2.2)	0.7
Yorkshire/Humberside	9.0 (9.0)	7.0 (7.4)	4.9 (4.9)	6.3 (5.3)	20.4 (19.9)	7.0 (6.5)	2.8
North-West	11.8 (11.7)	7.6 (9.0)	4.8 (5.3)	8.1 (8.5)	15.2 (15.7)	11.4 (4.4)	5.4
East Midlands	7.0 (7.1)	6.4 (6.5)	5.2 (4.4)	9.2 (11.8)	4.0 (3.5)	3.3 (0.0)	12.3
West Midlands	9.5 (9.5)	14.8 (16.8)	15.5 (15.0)	20.3 (21.5)	21.0 (25.7)	14.2 (16.3)	8.0
East Anglia	3.5 (3.5)	1.3 (1.2)	1.0 (1.0)	1.1 (0.5)	1.3 (1.1)	1.1 (1.1)	1.6
South-East	31.0 (31.1)	55.6 (52.2)	64.7 (66.7)	47.3 (48.8)	30.1 (23.3)	56.5 (67.4)	64.0
South-West	8.0 (8.1)	2.9 (2.0)	2.7 (2.1)	3.0 (1.1)	1.5 (1.1)	1.4 (0.0)	2.4
Number (1981)	54,814,500	2,207,245	545,744	673,704	295,461	64,561	181,321
Number (1983–5)	54,118,000	2,349,000	528,000	762,000	377,000	92,000	

[a] 1981 census and (in parentheses) Labour Force Survey (LFS) averages for 1983–5. These two sets of figures are not directly comparable.
[b] Census data refer to those in households where the head of household was born in the New Commonwealth or Pakistan. LFS data refer to those whose self-ascribed 'ethnic' category is not 'white'.
[c] LFS grouping: census designation is 'Caribbean'.
[d] LFS figures include people born in East Africa.
[e] LFS does not distinguish East Africans.
(Smith, 1989, Table 3, pp.28 & 29)

Table 13.2 Population distribution within the metropolitan regions of England

Region	% of regional population						
	Non-NCWP	All NCWP	Caribbean	Indian	Pakistani	Bangladeshi	East African
North							
Tyne & Wear	37.0	43.3	36.3	46.9	33.6	65.9	40.1
Elsewhere	63.0	56.7	63.7	53.1	66.4	34.1	59.9
Yorkshire/Humberside							
South Yorkshire	27.1	15.9	27.2	9.5	14.8	13.8	12.0
West Yorkshire	40.9	76.7	69.9	81.4	84.0	70.2	72.2
Elsewhere	32.0	7.4	2.9	9.1	1.2	16.0	15.8
North-West							
Greater Manchester	40.1	59.3	77.6	54.5	57.1	73.5	60.9
Merseyside	24.0	8.8	9.9	6.2	1.6	6.0	5.6
Elsewhere	35.9	31.9	12.5	39.3	41.3	20.5	33.5
West Midlands							
West Midlands MC	49.1	87.4	91.2	88.2	88.5	89.9	79.7
Elsewhere	50.9	12.6	8.8	11.8	11.5	10.1	20.3
South-East							
Greater London	37.1	77.0	86.9	70.2	58.8	79.1	78.1
Elsewhere	62.9	23.0	13.1	29.8	41.2	20.9	21.9
Total in metropolitan counties	47.9	78.8	88.1	74.9	74.4	81.0	77.4
Total elsewhere in metropolitan region	52.1	21.2	11.9	25.1	25.6	19.0	22.6
% in England in metropolitan regions	77.9	89.1	91.0	86.2	92.8	94.0	83.2

Census data: based on persons resident in private households with head of household born in the NCWP (see note 1).
(ibid., Table 4, p.31)

Table 13.3 Models of intervention to achieve racial justice

	Model 1	Model 2	Model 3	Model 4
Point of intervention	Individual	Individual	Group	Group
Principle of intervention	*Rights* Securing economic efficiency, preserving property rights	*Rights* Securing universal rights of citizenship: political, civil and social	*Needs* Meeting general economic needs	*Needs* Meeting special needs A Technical B 'Structural'
Means of intervention	Market deregulation plus minimum state subsidy for those medically or legally out of the workforce	State provisioning in cash or kind	Vertical (income) redistribution	Horizontal redistribution A B To cope with To compensate for age, illness sate for and handicap disadvantage and discrimination
Criteria for judging success	Economic prosperity, equal opportunity in the market place, fully protected property rights	Egalitarianism: an extension of effective rights to welfare, justice, political participation and employment	Equality of outcome in material circumstances	A B Attainment Attainment of minimum of quotas of standards representation through equity[a] or privilege[b]

[a] The guarantee that like cases are treated alike.
[b] Forms of positive discrimination (see text).
(ibid., Table 6, p.187)

14

Inequality and Segregation in Northern Ireland

D. Smith and G. Chambers (1991), *Inequality in Northern Ireland*, Oxford, Clarendon Press.

Nicholas Abercrombie

Introduction

Northern Ireland is seldom out of the news. What produces the headlines are terrorist incidents in the province itself or on the mainland. This violent conflict in Northern Ireland is often interpreted as being entirely about religion – as a modern version of a religious war between Protestants and Catholics. This book, while hardly denying the religious dimension, looks instead at the relationship between conflict and *social inequality*.

Recent History and the Social Context

In 1922 the statelet of Northern Ireland was created, guaranteeing a perpetual Protestant and unionist majority. As the state was established, Protestant power became entrenched in all the major institutions. In proportion to their numbers, Protestants were overrepresented in the public services and, in general, had a substantial advantage in employment and earnings. Unionists (those who believe in the continued union with the rest of Great Britain rather than the rest of Ireland and who are almost invariably Protestant) had a monopoly of power in regional government and, through manipulation of the franchise and of electoral boundaries, controlled a disproportionate number of local authorities which were then run on sectarian lines discriminating against Catholics. In 1968, however, there was mounting political pressure from civil rights organizations and from the government on the mainland, which resulted in a number of reforms being introduced by the unionist Northern Ireland government.

These reforms antagonized the Protestant supporters of the unionist government who saw themselves losing their earlier privileges. As a result, the government was replaced by direct rule from Westminster in 1972. The reforms continued however and serious attempts were made to remove discrimination against Catholics in the public services, housing, and employment. Local government was reformed and extensive changes were made to the police and the security services. Following these developments, there was a widespread view that discrimination had been removed and that there was equality of opportunity between Protestants and Catholics.

Catholics form a minority in Northern Ireland, though a large one, making up between 37.6% and 38.6% of the population in 1981. It goes almost without saying that religion matters. 80% of the population claim that they are members of a church, compared with 13% on mainland Britain. Similarly, 70% go to church regularly compared to 21% on the mainland. The education system is still largely segregated on religious lines. For example, in the 1970s in 95% of state schools the proportion of Catholics was under 5%, while in 98% of Catholic voluntary schools the proportion of Protestants was also less than 5%.

Methods

Smith and Chambers' study was set up under the auspices of the Policy Studies Institute which had been asked by the Standing Advisory Commission of Human Rights in Northern Ireland to mount an investigation of inequality, discrimination, and segregation in the province. Four main sources of data were used. First, the main source of information on the pattern of employment, unemployment, and housing was a Continuous Household Survey for 1983–5 which was carried out by the Northern Ireland government. The authors carried out a secondary analysis of these data which were based on interviews with almost 10,000 households and over 21,000 individuals. Second, in order to investigate the policies and practices at various workplaces, the authors carried out a series of interviews at a representative sample of 260 workplaces throughout Northern Ireland. This study was supplemented by 12 more detailed case-studies. Third, to study the perceptions that the population of Northern Ireland had of their society, a survey of a representative sample of some 1700 adults was carried out. Lastly, the condition of the housing stock and the methods of allocating council housing were investigated by a re-analysis of an existing survey and a study of council house waiting lists.

Principal Findings

(i) *Violence*

Perhaps surprisingly, Northern Ireland is one of the least crime-prone areas of Great Britain and, intriguingly, people feel safer there than in mainland Britain. As *Table 14.1*, p.161 shows, deaths and injuries from civil disturbances including acts of terrorism, are outweighed by those from road accidents. Nonetheless, it is clear that violence, and the fear of violence, has a major impact on everyday life in the province. Just under half of those surveyed by Smith and Chambers had known someone killed in terrorist violence while 11% had had a relative killed. The number of terrorist incidents reported varies from area to area. It is highest in Catholic areas and declines as the proportion of Protestants increases. This is, no doubt, related to the different ways in which the paramilitary groups work. The Catholic, or nationalist, paramilitaries (the IRA for example) attack members of the security forces as well as Protestant paramilitaries or civilians. The Protestant, or unionist, paramilitaries (the UDF for example), on the other hand, only attack members of the IRA or Catholic civilians. As a result, a larger number of Catholic civilians are killed.

(ii) *Segregation*

Hostility between ethnic or religious groups is often said to be partly related to how segregated they are – how little they are able to mix and interact together in their everyday lives. Smith and Chambers investigated the degree of segregation between the Protestant and Catholic communities in Northern Ireland by studying where people lived and worked, how friendships were formed, and even whether people felt confident about travelling outside their neighbourhood.

A substantial minority (38%) of Protestants believe that they live in areas which are almost totally Protestant, while a smaller proportion of Catholics (11%) inhabit communities which largely exclude Protestants. Some difference in the degree to which the two communities are segregated is bound to occur since there are more Protestants than Catholics. Allowing for this, however, Protestants do live in more segregated conditions. Any individual Protestant is more likely to live with members of his or her own group than is a Catholic. Partly because the populations of the two religions are not evenly spread, the pattern of segregation varies across the province. However, Belfast is even more segregated than one might expect, with Catholics tending to keep to their own communities as much as Protestants. In middle class areas, on the contrary, there is much greater mixing of the religious faiths.

There is therefore substantial residential segregation in Northern Ireland. Separation of the two religious communities does penetrate even further into everyday life. For example, residential segregation might well mean that, to a certain extent, people do not travel outside their religious community. To test the degree of this kind of segregation, Smith and Chambers asked their respondents about their mobility. Overall, 23% said that they avoided going into the opposite community, 66% said that they went at some time but only 19% went often.

One of the fundamental tests of the degree of segregation in any population is whether families remain separate or become intermixed through marriage. In Northern Ireland there is a very high degree of segregation in this respect. Asked what community their grandparents belonged to, the great majority named the same community as themselves (95% for Protestants and 88% for Catholics). Very high proportions – 98% for Protestants and 95% for Catholics – marry within their own group. There is some evidence that this pattern is breaking down since there is more inter-marriage among the younger age groups.

Segregation also persists in friendships though, as one might expect, to a lesser extent. About three-quarters of Protestants and 60% of Catholics say that all or most of their friends belong to their community. However, the proportion of those who say that all of their friends belong to their group is fairly small – 25% for Protestants and 18% for Catholics. Young Protestants show less segregation in their friendships than their elders although the same is not true for Catholics.

The last area of segregation to be considered is that of the work-place. In general, work-places are less segregated than residential areas or families and friends. Smith and Chambers' findings suggest that about one third of work-places are highly segregated having 95% or more of the workforce drawn from one community. When asked for their attitudes to integration of workplaces, the majority of respondents said that they did not mind a completely mixed workforce. On the other hand, the *area* in which the workplace is situated did have a more powerful effect. A majority said that they would avoid making an application to a company in an area of the opposite group. Respondents are much more concerned about the areas in which their workplace is situated than they are about the religious balance of the workplace itself. This suggests that 'enemy territory' is defined in terms of residential areas.

(iii) *Employment and unemployment*

A substantial source of inequality in any society is access to gainful employment. Catholics have a much higher rate of unemployment than Protestants. In the period 1983–5, the rate among Catholics was 35.1% while among the Protestant community it was 14.9%. Smith and Chambers spend some considerable effort in trying to explain this difference by looking in turn at a number of possible causal factors. One possibility is that the two communities are differently represented in different socio-economic groups. For example, 34% of employed Protestants are in the non-manual categories while only 22% of Catholics are. Since non-manual workers have lower rates of unemployment, this might help to account for the greater tendency of Catholics to unemployment. In fact, Smith and Chambers show that for *any* socio-economic group, Catholics have higher rates of unemployment.

They apply the same technique to other possible factors. The Catholic population tends to be younger and young people are more likely to be unemployed. Again the differences between the two communities remain after controlling for age, that is, for any age group there is still a difference in rates of unemployment. Similar results are obtained for the type of industry (Catholics disproportionately work in high unemployment industries like construction) and level of qualification (Catholics tend to have lower levels of vocational qualifications). The benefits system is also examined in that, since Catholics have larger families on the whole and therefore have higher levels of benefit, it has been argued that there is a disincentive to seek paid work. Again, however, Protestant and Catholic families of similar size still have greatly different rates of unemployment.

Smith and Chambers' method of explaining unemployment relies so far on isolating a number of possible factors and seeing if they are *individually* responsible for differences in unemployment rates. It might, however, be possible that these factors *interacting* together might explain the difference. Using a logistic regression model, which tests for interactions of variables, Smith and Chambers show that this is not so. The difference in unemployment rates persists. Their conclusion is that there is discrimination against Catholics who therefore have their *opportunities* for employment restricted. This conclusion is examined in more detail below.

The fact that Catholics have higher rates of unemployment is bound to mean that, as a whole, their standard of living is lower. This inequality is made more pronounced by a number of other factors. First, a higher proportion of Protestant than of Catholic women are in work, so a higher proportion of Protestant households will contain two wage earners. Second, Protestant families tend to be smaller on average. Third, Protestants tend to have jobs at higher levels than Catholics. Thus, within any occupation, Protestants will occupy more of the promoted positions. It is true that there are slight differences in levels of qualifications between the two communities but these are not great enough to explain the differences in job level. Lastly, Catholics tend to work less overtime.

(iv) *Discrimination*

Since there are no other features of the Catholic population that would make them have a higher rate of unemployment, it seems logical to conclude that discrimination of a sort is responsible. Discrimination can be either informal or formal. That is, employers may deliberately exclude Catholics, from good intentions or bad. Or they may behave in such a way that Catholics are excluded, for example by the display of Protestant regalia or posters advocating the Unionist cause. Discrimination in either case is notoriously difficult to prove in that it involves very detailed investigation of actual employment practices as they occur. Smith and Chambers were unable to do this so they concentrated on two other methods of investigating discrimination. First, they asked people whether they thought that there was discrimination at work. Second, they carried out a study of work-places to see how, or whether, *anti-discrimination* legislation was working.

Protestants and Catholics differ greatly in their estimates of the likelihood of employment. 56% of Catholics, compared with 9% of Protestants, say that Protestants have a better chance of finding a job. A possible explanation of this very large difference is that unemployment has become a symbol of the dispute between the two communities about social justice. To follow this up, respondents were asked a series of questions about the likelihood of people in Northern Ireland being refused a job because of their religion. A summary of their responses appears as *Table 14.2*, p.161. Responses vary widely depending on what kind of employer is being considered. A majority of respondents think that there are small businesses that discriminate. Smaller numbers think that there are larger businesses and local councils that discriminate. Relatively few (17%) consider that the civil service discriminates. There are differences between the communities in their responses. For small businesses and the civil service the differences are relatively small, with Catholics in general being more likely to believe that discrimination occurs. In larger businesses and local councils, on the other hand, the differences are much greater.

The belief that discrimination occurs is therefore fairly widespread. However, one cannot assume that everybody, Protestants and Catholics alike, believes that it is the *minority* group that suffers. It is possible that Protestants believe that discrimination is directed against them. To a large extent this is confirmed by Smith and Chambers' study in that many respondents interpret discrimination in terms of *territory*. That is, they believe that Catholics are discriminated against when they wish to work in a Protestant area and Protestants are similarly treated when applying for work in Catholic territory. Protestants have a greater tendency to adopt territorial explanations of discrimination but there is a substantial minority of Catholics who believe that they are discriminated against *as* Catholics.

In their study of workplaces Smith and Chambers aimed, largely by asking managers, to investigate how far companies had implemented fair, non-discriminatory, employment policies. In a number of respects, the policies of most employers were such that discrimination could easily occur. First, the great majority of employers said that fair employment legislation had little effect on them. Second, most employers did not have the objective of achieving a workforce balanced between the two communities. They said, either that no useful purpose would be served by such a policy, or that they simply aimed to employ the best person for the job.

Third, job recruitment was, for the majority of the firms, very informal, depending on word of mouth, recommendation from current employees, or trade union nomination. Such recruitment methods are bound to increase the numbers drawn from any one community. Lastly, very few companies had formal policies on discrimination or methods of monitoring or dealing with it.

(v) *The public services and housing*

There is, therefore, at least the potential for employment discrimination and substantial numbers of people believe there to be such discrimination. Some parts of the public sector seem to be exceptions however. For example, public sector employers are more likely to be aware of relevant legislation, to have anti-discrimination policies, and to use formal methods of recruitment – open advertising, formal interviews – which are less likely to be discriminatory. As a result perhaps, people see the public services as relatively fair employers. For example, the proportion of respondents who think that the civil service discriminates is much smaller than for other employers.

The public sector in Northern Ireland is, of course, not only important as an employer. It also provides services of all kinds, one of the most important of which is housing. Is the allocation of public housing fair?

To determine this question, Smith and Chambers compared those allocated public housing throughout 1987 with those on the waiting list as it stood at the end of 1987. Using this method it seems that the chances of Catholics receiving public housing were lower than those for Protestants. However, one also has to take into account housing *need*. The allocation system is not supposed to treat everybody equally; it is supposed to benefit those in greatest housing need. In fact, Catholics tend to have *greater* housing need, which suggests that they are at an even greater disadvantage in the allocation system. Furthermore, although the houses on Catholic estates are no worse in basic design, they are in a much worse state of repair.

All this suggests that there is a measure of discrimination against Catholics in the allocation of public housing. However, it is not all that great and the respondents in Smith and Chambers' survey from both communities tended to agree that the allocation system was, on the whole, fair.

(vi) *Perceptions of the Troubles*

The problems of Northern Ireland have often been seen in constitutional terms; the issue is whether the province should remain as part of the United Kingdom or whether it should become part of a united Ireland. Smith and Chambers were interested to find out what the population thought were the causes of the Troubles. In fact, social issues – discrimination, civil rights, the economic situation – were mentioned as causes as often as political and constitutional issues. The two communities have different views of what causes the Troubles. Protestants are more likely to see constitutional questions and violence itself as the main causes while Catholics are more likely to mention civil rights or discrimination. Nonetheless, in Smith and Chambers' view, these differences in views of the causes of the conflict are less important than the similarities.

Evaluation

Smith and Chambers' study is an exhaustive investigation of aspects of inequality and discrimination. It succeeds in showing clearly how the two communities are segregated and how Catholics are not only unequal in condition but also have unequal opportunities, especially in employment. Three aspects of the study somewhat limit the *general* conclusions that can be drawn from it. First, the main reason for inequality is assumed to be discrimination. There are, however, no *direct* tests of such discrimination. A standard way of providing a test in employment, for instance, is to send two actors who are identically qualified, but from different communities, for the same job. Smith and Chambers admit the necessity of such tests but say that they are not possible in the Northern Ireland situation. Without them, however, they are forced to speculate that discrimination actually occurs. Second, the study focuses largely on unemployment as a source of inequality. While it is undoubtedly true that employment opportunities are a major source of different life-chances, a more rounded picture of inequality would have been useful. For example, an account of inequalities in health, in income and wealth, and a more detailed analysis of education and employment status, would have completed the picture. Lastly, one of the aims of the study was to look at the perceptions that the people of Northern Ireland had of their society. While this is an admirable aim in itself, the authors frequently use perceptions as evidence for the existence of a phenomenon. Again, it would have been useful to have more systematic comparisons of what people perceived to be the case, with what other kinds of evidence revealed.

Conclusion

Three important conclusions emerge from Smith and Chambers' study. First, they demonstrate the great importance of territory. Protestants and Catholics have a strong sense of the area in which they live and a corresponding sense of 'enemy territory'. This sense of place determines a whole range of other attitudes and behaviour. Secondly, there is an inequality of condition between Protestants and Catholics represented, among other features, by the higher rate of unemployment among Catholics. Lastly, the explanation of this continuing inequality seems likely to be that Catholics suffer from discrimination in employment.

Appendices

Table 14.1 Deaths and injuries: civil disturbances compared with road accidents

	Civil disturbances		Road accidents	
	Killed	Injured	Killed	Seriously injured
1969	13	n.a.	257	1,419
1970	25	n.a.	n.a.	n.a.
1971	174	2,543	304	2,135
1972	487	4,876	372	2,430
1973	250	2,651	335	2,358
1974	216	2,398	316	2,268
1975	247	2,474	313	2,231
1976	297	2,729	300	2,570
1977	112	1,398	355	2,905
1978	81	985	288	2,749
1979	113	875	293	2,546
1980	75	801	229	2,387
1981	101	1,350	223	2,418
1982	97	525	216	2,503
1983	77	510	173	2,300
1984	64	866	189	2,465
1985	54	916	177	1,148
1986	61	1,450	236	1,825
1987	93	1,130	214	1,884
1971–87	2,599	26,477	4,533	39,122

(Smith and Chambers, 1991, Table 2.3, p.40)

Table 14.2 Views on discrimination in recruitment to employment, by religion (%)

	Total	Protestants	Catholics
Small businesses			
Often discriminate	27	27	28
Ever discriminate	63	64	62
They do discriminate and this is always wrong	36	33	43
Larger businesses			
Often discriminate	17	9	33
Ever discriminate	40	28	60
They do discriminate and this is always wrong	31	19	51
The Civil Service			
Often discriminate	7	6	9
Ever discriminate	17	14	21
They do discriminate and this is always wrong	13	10	19
Local councils			
Often discriminate	18	14	25
Ever discriminate	39	35	44
They do discriminate and this is always wrong	30	24	40
Base: all	*1,672*	*1,059*	*594*

(ibid., Table 5.29, p.217)

Acknowledgements

The authors and publishers would like to thank the following for permission to reproduce copyright material:

Oxford University Press and Robert Erikson and John Goldthorpe for tables from *The Constant Flux: a Study of Class Mobility in Industrial Societies*; Routledge and Michael Savage *et al.*, for the table and figure from *Property, Bureaucracy, and Culture; Middle Class Formation in Contemporary Britain*; Unwin Hyman and G. Marshall *et al.*, for the tables and questionnaire extract from *Social Class in Modern Britain*; Unwin Hyman and Peter Saunders for the tables from *A Nation of Home Owners*; Unwin Hyman and Rosemary Crompton and Kay Sanderson for the table from *Gendered Jobs and Social Change*; Routledge and Anne Witz for the figure from *Professions and Patriarchy*; Macmillan Press Ltd. and Sarah Whatmore for the extracts from *Farming Women: gender, work and family enterprise*; Macmillan Press Ltd. and Sheila Allen and Carol Wolkowitz for the table from *Homeworking: myths and realities*; Oxford University Press and Vaughan Robinson for the table and figures from *Transients, Settlers and Refugees*; Blackwell/Polity Press and Susan J. Smith for the tables from *The Politics of 'Race' and Residence*; Oxford University Press and D. Smith and G. Chambers for the tables from *Inequality in Northern Ireland*.

Every effort has been made to obtain permissions but the publishers would be pleased to hear from any unacknowledged source and full acknowledgement will be made at the first opportunity.